REQUIEM FOR
A CLASSIC

REQUIEM FOR A CLASSIC

Thanksgiving Turkey Day Classic

Thurman W. Robins, Ed. D.

authorHOUSE®

AuthorHouse™
1663 Liberty Drive
Bloomington, IN 47403
www.authorhouse.com
Phone: 1-800-839-8640

First published by AuthorHouse   08/02/2011

ISBN: 978-1-4634-0976-0 (sc)
ISBN: 978-1-4634-0975-3 (hc)
ISBN: 978-1-4634-0974-6 (ebk)

Library of Congress Control Number: 2011910723

Printed in the United States of America

Contents

Dedication

This book is dedicated to my daughters Emma, Thelma and Kelley. It is also dedicated to all former Wheatley and Yates teachers, coaches and administrators, along with all the students who attended both schools during the period of segregation.

Acknowledgements

Thanks to all of the individuals who encouraged me to write this book including many of my high school classmates and friends: Thelma Robins Gould, Freddie Gould, Deloris Johnson, Donald Dickson, Napoleon Johnson, Carolyn O'Neal Baugh, Jeanette Bryant Vinson, Richard Nichols, Robert and Gertrude Dean Robins, Myron and Catherin Robins, Frances Jackson, Eugene Floyd, Robert and Barbara Brown, Darrell Jones, Pete Hillard and Carl Anderson. Thanks to my colleagues Mitchell Allen, Kenyatta Cavil, Jay Cummings, James Cunningham, James Douglas, Jesse Hurst, Franklin Jones, Joyce Jones, Claudette Ligons, Walter McCoy, Henry North, Danita Bailey-Perry, Launey Roberts, and Carroll Robinson, for their encouragement.

A special thanks to my wife for her continued support throughout this process. Her patience, encouragement and support made the project possible. A very special thanks to Dr. Clarise Lowe for her guidance, thoughtful input, suggestions, recommendations and editing of the manuscript.

Last but certainly not least, I would like to thank the Library staffs of Texas Southern University and the University of Houston for their valuable assistance, resources and materials. Thanks also to Georgia Provost for the photos provided.

Foreword

**Forgiveness means letting go of a hurtful situation
and moving on with your own happiness.
—Amanda Ford—**

This book was written especially for those individuals who grew up during the era of segregation, their offspring, and anyone else who desires to know the rich history of a community of people who had little in the way of financial means, but were rich in those things which provide substance for a lifetime.

The impetus for writing the book sprang largely from a conversation among 2007 inductees of the Texas Black Sports Hall of Fame and interested individuals of the Houston community gathered at the inductees' breakfast in Dallas. Most of the individuals knew of Jack Yates and Phillis Wheatley High Schools, but were unaware of their epic Thanksgiving Day football battles which took place during the period of segregation.

Much of the information contained herein came from interviews with former students of Jack Yates and Phillis Wheatley High Schools. However, accounts of parades, pep rallies and game highlights of the 1950s are personal recollections of the author. The author also summarized game write-ups which appeared in *The Houston Informer, Houston Press, Houston Post, Houston Chronicle, Forward Times* newspapers from 1927 through 1966.

Segregation and Jim Crow laws came into existence following the Civil War during the period of Reconstruction and lasted into the middle 1960s throughout most of the United States. A few northern states allowed some flexibility in applying segregation laws. However, the southern states were more rigid in staunchly observing them in all aspects of society, including accommodations, transportation, education, and social events. Nearly all public schools in the south were separated according to race. There was little to no mixing of races in these schools or in any activities sponsored by the schools.

A Supreme Court decision in 1896 was the basis for public education's remaining separate along racial lines. The separate-but-equal ruling of Plessy vs. Ferguson subscribed to the doctrine that "legislation is powerless to eradicate racial instincts" and laid down the "separate but equal" rule for the justification of continued segregation. Integration of public schools did not become a reality in southern states until well into the middle 1960s. Federal court orders forced nearly all public school districts in America to integrate their school systems. The 1954 Supreme Court decision rendered in Brown vs. the Board of Education began the process of public school integration. As a result, the Houston Independent School District (HISD) was forced to begin integration of its schools by forced federal court order beginning in 1962. Its initial procedure was to integrate one grade level per year, beginning with the first grade, until full integration was achieved. However, in 1967 this policy was eliminated, and all grade levels were integrated.

Inasmuch as Booker T. Washington High School was already in existence and Jack Yates High School and Phillis Wheatley High School were created in 1926 and 1927 respectively, they existed under the laws of the land, which upheld the segregation providing the backdrop for all school activities. Students, parents and citizens of the Black community had no alternative other than to operate under the separate-but-equal doctrine forced upon them. Nevertheless, Blacks strived to provide the best education and extracurricular experiences possible for their children. The wholesome rivalries which evolved among these three Black high schools of the era were fostered by the system. The administrative leadership of Booker T. Washington, Phillis Wheatley, and Jack Yates High Schools provided continuity and stability within the schools and their communities. This leadership and the school faculties helped to instill ethical principles and moral values within students. In addition, students were encouraged to strive for excellence and to be the best that each could be.

The facilities of the three Black high schools were adequate, but had by no means been created equal to the Reagans, San Jacintos, Austins, and other white high schools of that era. Much of the equipment, study materials and financial resources was not equal. Textbooks and pupils' desks discarded by the white schools were sent to Black schools, a discrepancy that was of primary concern in the Black community. Rarely, if ever, did black students receive new equipment. The team uniforms and athletic equipment were also often secondhand. Practice fields were less than adequate and by no stretch of the imagination up to the standards of the day. One exception was the playing fields used for football games and other athletic contests. All HISD schools played their football games at the same facilities, either at Barrs Field, East End Park, Buffalo Stadium, or HISD's public school stadium. Inasmuch as the white schools had first preference for dates, Black schools seldom had use of the facilities on weekends.

The use of materials and secondhand equipment continued well into the 1960s. Because of the ever increasing number of Black pupils in HISD which began during the late 1940s and continued throughout the early to mid 1950s, HISD administration had to create additional Black high schools as the three original schools were suffering from overcrowding. Kashmere Gardens High School opened in 1957, and E.E. Worthing High School opened in 1958. A new Wheatley High School facility had been built in 1949, and new buildings were constructed for Jack Yates High School in 1958 and for Booker T. Washington High School in 1959.

Even after these new school facilities opened, and these schools participated in the athletic programs of the previously existing Black schools, no contest could overshadow the Yates vs. Wheatley rivalry with its annual Thanksgiving Day football game. As attendance grew, numerous festivities were added, and more and more loyal alumni returned for this "homecoming" The Yates-Wheatley "match-up" became a Classic, entrenched in the community's observation of Thanksgiving. The attendance at this classic event continued to draw increasingly large audiences until its demise in 1966.

The Yates vs. Wheatley Thanksgiving Day Classic was an event which grew to glorious heights during the period of segregation. The Classic was a social as well as an athletic contest which engulfed the entire Houston Black community. It was a celebration, a significant prideful "happening" created and nourished not only by the schools and alumni, but by the majority of Houston's Black citizens, and during the height of its glory, by the many white sports fans who attended as well.

The Classic's demise came swiftly and abruptly as change often does. However, many young boys and girls of that era had been profoundly influenced by its existence. It was a sterling example of what was good, productive and significant in the Black schools and community of Houston.

Introduction

WHERE DID THE GAME GO?

**Always concentrate on how far you have come,
rather than how far you have left to go.
The difference in how easy it seems will amaze
you.
—Heidi Johnson—**

Each year the entire community anticipated with great joy another Thanksgiving Day Football Classic between Yates and Wheatley High Schools. Oh! What a glorious time! What a magnificent happening for the community. The Classic was rich in pageantry, glamour, splendor and entertainment. Boys and girls, men and women, old and young sports fans all looked forward to this day when the high schools from Third Ward and Fifth Ward faced off against each other in another thrilling football contest. The sheer spectacle of it all—parades, floats, "dressed-to-kill" fans, shiny, fancy automobiles, pre- and post-game dances, and the most exciting climax of it all, the game itself. The Thanksgiving Day Yates vs. Wheatley football game was the social, cultural, entertaining, sporting event of the year for the entire Black community of Houston. Throngs of fans, both black and white, turned out to witness this Classic each year,

Before 1947 there were few Black collegiate football games in the city proper. Texas State University for Negroes, now Texas Southern University (TSU), came into existence in 1947, and most citizens were slow to develop allegiance; therefore, attendance at its football games was somewhat small in comparison to that of the local high school games. However, the local high schools had begun team sports during the 1920s, and Colored High School fielded football teams in the early part of the century.

Colored High School, established in 1893, was renamed Booker T. Washington High School in 1926. When Jack Yates and Phillis Wheatley High Schools were established in the late 1920s, the three schools began playing each other, and natural rivalries developed. Most of the Black citizenry identified with the high school located in the community in which they resided: Jack Yates in the Third Ward; Booker T. Washington, in the Fourth Ward; and Phillis Wheatley in the Fifth Ward. The Thanksgiving Day holiday game meant a great deal to the Black community. It was the single event which brought people of different persuasions together on this day. Mothers, fathers, grandmothers, grandfathers, cousins, aunts and uncles and a host of friends and foes gathered to witness this long-awaited contest and to share similar experiences. From its inception through the mid 1940s, the Thanksgiving Day game rotated among the three Black schools.

An article in the third edition of *The Houston Informer* (December 3, 1927), had headlines which read, "Golden Eagles Claw Wildcats on Turkey Day". The article also reported, "It took the entire half of the boys on West Dallas to recover from their first shock and realize what a calamity it would be to be defeated by a team playing their first season, and when they did wake up, it wasn't long then. The game ended 19 to 12 in favor of Washington's Golden Eagles."

The game between Jack Yates and Phillis Wheatley had its beginning in 1927; however, this first meeting did not occur on Thanksgiving Day. In the beginning contests among the three schools, Jack Yates played Wheatley on Armistice Day, Wheatley played Washington on Thanksgiving Day, and Yates played Washington on Christmas Day. However, in 1939 with the reorganization of the Texas Interscholastic League for Colored Schools (TILCS) the district playoff format was established, and the Christmas Day games were eliminated. As a result, these three schools rotated play on Thanksgiving Day. After several years of rotation it became clear that the Yates vs. Wheatley game drew larger attendance than any other pairing. Larger attendance meant greater revenue for HISD.

In the early 1940s, Yates' principal, William Holland, and Wheatley's principal, John Coldwell, began lobbying to eliminate the rotation. HISD administration ended the rotation in 1947, the year which marked the beginning of the Turkey Day Classic between Yates and Wheatley on Thanksgiving Day. The last game played on Thanksgiving Day was November 24, 1966, with Yates claiming the victory.

Why did it all end? Integration! Integration of the public schools in Houston and in many parts of Texas brought about the end of this glorious affair on Thanksgiving Day. Prior to integration all Black schools in Texas were governed by the TILCS commonly referred to as the Prairie View Interscholastic League (PVIL). All other schools in Texas were governed by the University Interscholastic League (UIL). With integration all public school competition in Texas was governed by the regulations of the UIL. The UIL rules and district playoff format mandated that all district games be completed before Thanksgiving Day.

This reorganization brought an end to the glorious game so many dearly loved. There would be no more breakfast dances, Thanksgiving Day parades, or any of the other festive galas and events associated with this day. What a bummer! What a tragedy! The traditions established over 39 years ago had come to an abrupt end.

Most fans did not realize it at first, but to hold this contest between such rivals on any day other than Thanksgiving Day would not be the same. Only after the first non-Thanksgiving day contest in 1967 did the loyal fans of both schools realize that their beloved Classic was no more. The thrill was gone. In its place was an empty hollow within the hearts of Wheatley and Yates fans and alumni. Both the Third and Fifth Ward communities felt the emptiness of Thanksgiving without their beloved Classic. No parades, no dances, no pre-Thanksgiving breakfast, all spelled gloom and a sense of loss. It was as if a special family member was forever gone.

The absence of the Yates-Wheatley football game on Thanksgiving Day affected not only the fans as well as non-fans, for the Black community and the city as well suffered immensely from the game's demise. Many alumni of both schools had come from afar, the east coast, west coast and all other parts of the nation, to be with family and friends on this day. Merchants and business establishments over the entire city lost untold revenue. HISD and its athletics department lost its greatest revenue producer. For more than 20 years this contest had generated the largest income for HISD's athletic programs, more than any other game played by any of the city's schools. The City of Houston's bus and transportation department lost projected revenues as no extra busses were chartered because of the cancelation of the game. Tax revenue for the city also suffered as many tax dollars paid by merchants went uncollected because no game was played. The entire City of Houston felt immediately the economic, psychological and sociological impact of the absence of the Thanksgiving Day Classic. The anticipated joy, thrill and excitement of a Thanksgiving Day game between Yates and

Wheatley was to be no more. This was the end of an era, the demise of a Classic.

Many football fans have expressed their views that the Yates vs. Wheatley football game on Thanksgiving Day made the holiday seem complete. Without the battle between the Fifth and Third Ward schools the holiday was incomplete. For nearly 40 years the cross-town rivals had fought epic battles for the City of Houston bragging rights. The pomp and ceremony, glory, and splendor of the game and associated activities were lost forever. This, the major social event for the entire Black community, ended with integration of the Houston public schools. What a great price to pay for integration! In spite of this, most citizens, Blacks included, viewed integration as progress for the Black community.

In an interview with *The Houston Informer in* 1966, prior to the last Classic, Coaches Patterson of Yates and Walker of Wheatley commented regarding their feelings. Coach Walker said, "I enjoyed the Annual Thanksgiving Game a little more than anyone else" (November 26, 1966). As a member of the Wheatley team, Walker had played in the Thanksgiving Day game in the second half of the 1930s. He continued, "It's something I have been living with since I was a player, and I probably got more of a kick out of it than some of the kids."

Coach Patterson said, "Well, you can't stand in the way of progress. Next year we will be playing in one of the two zones set up for the Houston high schools. Competition for the city championship will be underway when this game is usually scheduled." With 14 wins, 7 losses and 2 ties Coach Patterson is said to have won more games in the series than any other head coach.

Sports fans, alumni, and citizens were polled for their feelings about the games demise. Homer McCoy (1966), a teacher at Yates and an alumnus said, "This is like closing a door on a tradition. Thanksgiving Day can never be the same. However, we must give way to progress, and we, as citizens, should never wish to hold onto any tradition that impedes progress" (November 26, 1966).

Nevertheless, we are without the Yates vs. Wheatley Thanksgiving Day Classic, which will live on forever in the memories of those who witnessed or were a part of this glorious tradition. The fans of both schools and the Black community of the city mourn the loss of their beloved Thanksgiving Day Classic.

Chapter 1

BOOKER T. WASHINGTON, JACK YATES AND PHILLIS WHEATLEY HIGH SCHOOLS: THE BEGINNING

Appreciate every moment of every day because in retrospect they will all have gone by too fast.
—M. Buchwald—

Booker T. Washington High School, formerly known as Colored High School, was established in 1893 in the Fourth Ward community. The first high school for Blacks in the city, it was renamed in 1928. The school was relocated from Fourth Ward to its present location in Independence Heights in 1959. Charles Atherton served as its first principal from 1893 until 1912. James D. Ryan served as the second principal from 1912 until 1926, when he was named the first principal of Jack Yates High School. Others who served as principal included William E. Miller, 1926 to 1938; Dr. Ira B. Bryant, 1938 to1957; Arthur L. Huckaby, 1957 to 1965, and Franklyn D. Wesley, 1965 to 2007.

During the early years after 1866, most Black citizens settled in Fourth Ward, which is now considered a part of downtown

Houston. As the Black population grew, its members began to migrate to the Third and Fifth Wards. Originally sparsely settled by Blacks, large numbers began to settle in Fifth Ward by the mid-1880s. Robb Walsh of *The Houston Press* described the 1930s era Fifth Ward as "one of the proudest black neighborhoods" in the United States. The Third Ward area also saw tremendous growth in its number of citizens during this era. As Fourth Ward declined in Black population, the Third and Fifth Wards increased, and many Black-owned businesses sprang up in these neighborhoods.

Jack Yates High School was established in February of 1926, beginning with 17 teachers and 600 students. The school was named after the Reverend John Henry "Jack" Yates, a former slave born in Virginia in1828. He was prominently involved in the education of Black Houstonians in the late 1800s, having helped establish the Houston Baptist Academy for Blacks. He was also a member of Antioch Baptist Church, the first Black Baptist Church in Houston, and was selected as its first pastor in 1868. Jack Yates High School first location was 2610 Elgin in the Third Ward community. The second high school for Black children in the city, its first principal was James D. Ryan, who had served as Booker T. Washington High School's second principal prior to his appointment at Yates High School. He served as principal until his death in 1941. William Holland, who was assistant principal-coach, succeeded Ryan as principal.

During the early 1950s the school became so overcrowded that seventh graders had to attend in two shifts, one in the early morning and one in the late afternoon. In 1956 the overcrowding became so acute that a campus annex located at nearby Allen Elementary school was opened to accommodate the seventh-graders. Yates moved to its present location in the fall of 1958, and Dr. John E. Codwell was transferred from Wheatley High School who served as principal until his retirement in1964. James Alexander succeeded him as principal, serving from 1964 to 1972. The original Jack Yates campus became Ryan Colored Junior High School in the fall of 1958, now Ryan Middle School.

Phillis Wheatley High School was established in 1927 as the third Black high school in Houston. When established, it was one of the largest Black high schools in the United States with 2,600 students and 60 teachers. The school was named for Phillis Wheatley, a female poet, born 1753 in Senegal. She was made a slave at age seven and was purchased by the Wheatley family of Boston, Massachusetts, who taught her to read and write and encouraged her to write poetry. Her writings helped create the genre of Black American literature.

During the 1940s Wheatley's first facility on Lyons Avenue became so overcrowded that students were required to attend in shifts. A new campus was opened in the fall of 1949 on a new 14-acre site at 4900 Market Street. The school was once described as, "the finest Negro high school in the South", with a 1,500 seat auditorium, a gymnasium, an industrial arts facility, and a swimming pool. The former campus became E.O. Smith Junior High School, now E.O. Smith Middle School, named for Wheatley's first principal. Dr. John E. Codwell, who served as head football coach under Ernest O. Smith, succeeded him as the second principal of the school. He remained there until his transfer to Jack Yates high school in 1958. William Moore assistant principal under Codwell succeed him as principal of Wheatley and remained principal until 1971.

The Ties That Bind

Jack Yates, Phillis Wheatley and Booker T. Washington High Schools, popularly known as Yates, Wheatley, and Washington, shared common values and goals. Their relationship to their communities was positive with significant influence on the lives of their constituents. Emerging from these schools have come influential personalities and national celebrities in the visual and performing arts, like the siblings Debbie, Phylicia, and "Tex" Allen of Jack Yates, and Hubert Laws the internationally renowned flutist of Phillis Wheatley. Also notable are Yates graduates active in city government: Judson Robinson Jr., Judson Robinson III, and Anthony Hall. Wheatley produced state senator Barbara Jordan, later a Congressional representative together with George "Mickey" Leland. Other graduates were state representatives "Al" Edwards and Harold Dutton, County Commissioner El Franco Lee, and City Attorney Otis King. Washington also produced a state representative, Senfronia Thompson. However, its most remarkable graduate was perhaps Hattie Mae Whiting White, who, refusing to be intimidated or threatened, became the first Black elected to the Houston Independent School District (HISD) School Board as a trustee. In recognition of her leadership, the current HISD administration building bears her name. The functioning of society and the people therein is greatly impacted by its government, religious, and educational institutions.

When one looks closely at these schools, it is clear that each has enjoyed a effective history of continuity, of capable administrators, and successful leadership which greatly impacted their communities. Similar core values and traditions were shared by these three Black communities. Each community was stable, and family histories were tied to each school as brothers, sisters, fathers and mothers shared the same school experiences.

Washington High School, established in 1893 as Colored High School, was the first black high school in Houston. Located in the Fourth Ward community, it was the chief rival of both Yates and Wheatley. Its students, alumni and friends, although competitors of both Yates and Wheatley, also shared many of the common goals, custom and traditions. The school's administration and leadership was stable and, to some extent, a model for both

Yates and Wheatley. From the time of each school's beginning, Washington in 1893, Yates in 1926, and Wheatley in 1927, these traditions, customs and values were passed on to succeeding generations of students.

One such tradition revolved around football. Attorney Jim Nabrit, then the sports editor for *The Houston Informer,* wrote, "Houston high schools monopolize all holidays in the fall and winter for their inner-city games, and the Yates-Wheatley game on Armistice Day, the Wheatley-Washington game on Thanksgiving Day, and the Yates-Washington game on Christmas Day are annual sporting events attracting huge throngs. Everyone interested in football sets these days apart for those games a year in advance" (December 5, 1931).

The Houston Informer reported an interview with a former principal of Yates, William Holland, concerning what was to be the last scheduled Thanksgiving Day game. Holland said, "The Yates-Booker T. Washington game was played on Christmas Day. The Christmas date with Washington was discontinued with the formation of the Negro Interscholastic League. Wheatley and Washington were playing Thanksgiving Day, but the Yates-Wheatley game was developing into the type of rivalry that could become a real Holiday Classic. So, the Yates-Wheatley game was moved to Thanksgiving Day." Holland went on to say, "The Yates-Wheatley game became a natural because of the intense rivalry between John (Codwell) and myself, We battled on the field, off the field, in the Superintendent's office, in the Athletic Director's office, on the streets, and in the alleys" (November 26, 1966).

Holland's statement that the Christmas Day game between Yates and Washington was discontinued because of the formation of the Negro Interscholastic League was not totally correct. The Texas Interscholastic League for Colored Schools (TILCS) actually began in 1920. The discontinuing of the Yates-Washington game on Christmas was due to the TILCS's efforts to eliminate mythical state championships in football and basketball; therefore, it formed districts, a division which led to a formal playoff system to determine true state championships.

According to Prairie View Interscholastic League Coaches Association records (2005), Andrew "Pat" Patterson, a young coach at Houston's Yates High School was the initiator of the structured organization of the TILCS in 1939. He persuaded Yates High School Principal William Holland to present his organizational plan to Prairie View A&M College Vice-Principal Dr. E. B. Evans. In the spring of 1939, at a regular meeting of the TILCS, at Prairie View College, it was voted to divide the state into districts and have bi-district play-offs, semi-finals and finals to determine a true state championship for the Class AA colored high schools. The restructured plan was inaugurated in the 1940 football season. The formation of the district play eliminated the Yates-Washington Christmas day game.

Moving the Yates-Wheatley game to Thanksgiving Day proved to be an immense success. The Yates vs. Wheatley Thanksgiving Day Classic was viewed with pride and held in high esteem. Moreover, the Black city football championship often rested upon the outcome of the contest. It was a foregone expectation that alumni of the schools in the Houston Black community would be attending the Thanksgiving Day Classic or would know someone attending the Classic, so that most began preparation for such participation months and months in advance. Because of the fact that the Classic had such wide spread community appeal and support, it became one of the most influential social events of the Houston community.

Chapter 2

THE MEN WHO LED

The ultimate measure of a man is not where he stands in moments of comfort and conveniences, but where he stands at times of challenge and controversy.
—Martin Luther King, Jr.—

The principals and coaches of the high schools were men who had outstanding leadership ability. They laid the foundation for excellence and led the way, overcoming many obstacles as a result of segregation and Jim Crow laws, always prodding their students to seek excellence. The principals encouraged and motivated teachers and students under their charge. Their responsibilities were great, and often times they had to solve difficult problems which faced the school and their communities. Situations frequently arose which called for the use of diplomacy, intelligence, patience, and integrity, and they knew full well that mistakes could be detrimental to the school and the community. These men were necessarily courageous as well as influential in their decision-making process. They led their schools and helped persuade others in the community to follow their lead as they went about the business of educating an underserved population during difficult times. Their efforts helped mold the lives of young people as well as provide a symbol of unity and educational excellence, which inevitably improved the quality of life in the community.

The coaches were also very good leaders. They had to be creative and innovative in many ways as they often had to deal with inferior equipment and facilities yet provide leadership for young maturing teenagers. Their influence and guidance was significantly important in providing structure, discipline and commitment to a team sport. These coaches had to be wise, yet shrewd as they dealt with young boys but also often times had to deal with parents and relatives who did not always agree with their tactics.

The High School Principals

James D. Ryan, First Principal of Jack Yates High School (1926-1940). James D. Ryan had a brilliant educational career. He was born in 1872 in Navasota, Texas, Grimes County, where he attended public school. At an early age he won by competitive examination an appointment to Prairie View College, from which he received his bachelor's degree in 1890. His early teaching career had stops at Third Ward schools for two years, and Second Ward schools for one year, after which he was transferred to Colored High School, later renamed Booker T. Washington High School, where he taught mathematics for many years. He succeeded Charles Atherton, first principal of Booker T. Washington (1893-1912), to serve as principal from 1912 to 1926. Many referred to Ryan as the "Dean of Negro Educators in Houston."

Ryan served as first principal of Jack Yates High School, which opened February 8, 1926, with 17 teachers. His educational preparation included graduate studies at the University of

Chicago, the University of California and Columbia University. He was also awarded an honorary Masters of Arts degree from Wiley College in Marshall, Texas, in 1927. In addition, he served as the 29th president of the Colored State Teachers Association. Ryan was known as a civic person as he was involved in community projects throughout his career. For 18 years he was superintendent of Trinity Methodist Episcopal Church Sunday School. He also served as a member of the church's Trustee Board for many years.

Ernest Ollington Smith, First Principal of Phillis Wheatley High School (1927-1945). Ernest Ollington Smith was born in Shelby, Alabama. He attended Slater High School in Birmingham, Alabama, and graduated with a bachelor's degree from Fisk Preparatory School in Nashville, Tennessee. He did further graduate work at the University of Colorado.

Early in his teaching career he was assigned principal of the Hollywood School in Houston. He was also principal at Brock and Francis Harper Elementary Schools. After some years at these schools he was then assigned to the position of principal of the junior-senior Phillis Wheatley High School in 1927. Within ten years Wheatley had grown to be the largest and "most outstanding accredited Negro High School" in the southwest with more than 2600 pupils, 60 teachers and a campus estimated to be worth over half a million dollars. Professor Smith also organized the first "city night school for Colored people" and was head of this work for 18 years. He is also credited with inventing the "Triple Shift" in education, which was known for handling crowded classes and overcrowded schools.

He was civic-minded and was heavily involved in community enterprises. He was a member of the Y.M.C.A. Committee of Management, National Association for the Advancement of

Colored People, Fifth Ward Civic Improvement Club, Pilgrim Congregational Church and many other organizations.

William Holland, Second Principal of Jack Yates High School (1941-1958). A native of Terra Haute, Indiana, born March 2, 1904, Holland received his formal elementary, high school and college education in Terra Haute, Indiana. He received his Bachelor of Science degree from Indiana State Teachers College in 1926. He also attended the University of Illinois and the University of Notre Dame in 1930. While at Notre Dame, he studied football under the late great Knute K. Rockne. He received a M.S. degree in high school administration from Indiana State College in 1933. He taught at Walden College in Nashville, Tennessee, from 1925-1926, and then Tennessee State College from 1926-1927 before coming to Jack Yates High School. He taught physical education and coached football in his first appointment at Yates. His teaching and coaching paved the way for his later elevation to the position of Assistant Principal-Coach. He was often described as an educator with rare ability, sound judgment and keen intellect.

Holland was very civic minded and took part in most Third Ward civic activities. He was a member of Wesley Chapel A.M.E. Church early in his career, but became affiliated with Trinity United Methodist Episcopal Church in later years. He was known for speaking his mind, which often times did not set well with higher ranking administrators and board members of HISD. He persistently demanded better resources, better facilities, equipment and materials from the school administration. His outspoken truth and constant demands for quality materials and resources and support ultimately cost him the principal's position at the opening of the new Yates building in 1958. He remained in the district as principal of Ryan Middle school until his retirement. He served as a HISD school board trustee after retirement.

Dr. John E. Codwell, Second Principal of Phillis Wheatley High School (1945-1958); Third Principal of Jack Yates High School (1958-1964). The only individual who had the distinction of serving as principal at both Phillis Wheatley and Jack Yates High Schools, Dr. Codwell assumed the duties of principal at Wheatley upon the retirement of E.O. Smith in 1945. As reported in *African American News & Issues,* Sept. 18, 2002, "Codwell had coached all sports at Wheatley for more than 15 years before replacing Prof. J.C. Sanders as assistant principal". Codwell had served as head football coach, having led the Wildcats in their first meeting against Yates in 1927. Once Codwell became principal, his coaches were Rutherford Countee, football; Collins Briggs, basketball; O.B. Williams, track and field, and Frank Walker, head baseball and assistant football coach. Frank Walker later succeeded Countee as head football coach and was credited with being the first Texas high school coach to record over 100 wins.

Codwell, a native Houstonian, attended Colored High School, now Booker T. Washington High School, and was a star athlete in football, track and field, basketball and baseball. Codwell became principal of Jack Yates at the beginning of the 1958 fall semester. He replaced long time friend and colleague William Holland, who was assigned principal at Ryan Junior High School. Dr. Codwell remained principal at Yates until 1964, when he was replaced by James R. Alexander, who had served as his assistant principal. Upon his leaving Yates, Dr. Codwell went to Atlanta, Georgia, where he worked at the Southern Association of Secondary Schools and Colleges, an accrediting agency.

William Moore, Third Principal of Wheatley High School (1958-1971). William Moore has been described as a leader who had character, honor, agility, mobility, persistence and spirit. Moore had served as assistant principal under Dr. Coldwell from 1944 until becoming principal in 1958. Prior to this appointment he had taught mathematics from 1938 until 1944. Moore received the B.S. degree from Fisk University in 1928 and the M.A. degree from the University of Michigan in 1948.

James Alexander, Fourth Principal at Jack Yates High School (1964-1972). James R. Alexander Sr. was born August, 1904, in Smith Chapel community of Timpson, Texas. Upon completion of public school training in Marshall, Texas, he took his undergraduate studies at Tuskegee, Alabama, where he was privileged to work as personal aide to George Washington Carver, the noted scientist.

He continued his studies at Cornell University in New York State, with a concentration in Commercial Trade Cooking, and was the first to introduce it as a vocational course at Delaware State University. He came to the Houston Independent School District in 1936 and worked at Booker T. Washington High School as a teacher of horticulture and Woodwork. A short period later he became the only teacher of commercial cooking (boys only) in HISD. He earned the M.Ed. in administration from Texas Southern University and in 1957 became Assistant Principal at Booker T. Washington. In 1959 he was appointed assistant principal at Jack Yates High School and later became principal in 1964, remaining in the position until his retirement in 1972.

Having been reared in the Christian faith and baptized in the Baptist Church, he did not limit his service to one area. He taught the Senior Men's Bible Class at Olivet Missionary Baptist Church for many years. He was also an ardent worker with the Big Brothers program and an avid promoter of athletic competition and sportsmanlike behavior. He participated in many professional and social organizations that enhanced growth and commitment. His activity in the Boy Scouts of America program was both profound and fulfilling.

Chapter 3

ELITE RING MASTERS: COACHES SUPREME

It takes chances to make changes.
—Danielle Ballentine—

Andrew Pat Patterson, the Hick /Hickmon

The year was 1954, and both schools had winning records. The winner would be crowned city champion. Win or lose, the Wildcats would represent the district in the state playoffs because their 10-0 record was best in district play. Wheatley scored first in the opening period when Melvin Goffney picked up a fumble and scampered 61 yards for the score. The extra point try was good. During the second quarter, Yates had a sustained drive of 59 yards to score on the passing of Willie Wheat and explosive runs by Calvin "The Great" Scott. Wheat passed to, Lewis, who scored, but the point-after try by Jones was wide. The score remained 7-6 in favor of Wheatley.

Late in the second quarter Yates had the ball deep within Wheatley territory. The Lions had advanced the ball to the seven-yard line, where the offense stalled, and it was now fourth down. The Wildcats' defense dug in as it was determined to keep the Lions out of the end zone. They were too close to the goal line to punt, too far for a squeeze play; the obvious strategy would be a pass play. Could they score a touchdown? Seven yards was a long way to go. Yates quarterback, Wheat, looked to the sidelines for a signal from Coach Patterson, and the expression on his face said "What should we do?" He got a signal, and the team huddled. What would the play be? What play had Coach Patterson called?

Coach Andrew "Pat" Patterson came to Yates in 1938 as head baseball and basketball coach as well as assistant football coach. He assumed the head football coaching position in 1940 as a result of Coach Develous Johnson's call to the military. An outstanding athlete who had excelled in basketball and baseball, Patterson had played football under Coach "Pop" Long at Wiley College. Wiley's football team had won the Negro National Championship with Patterson as quarterback in 1932.

After graduation Patterson played a couple of years of professional baseball before taking a coaching job in Galveston, where he was held in high regard by his coaching peers. During his tenure at Yates in 1939 he had observed that a formal playoff system was lacking to determine a state champion in football and basketball. He began to devise a system which he would then recommend to his principal for consideration by the Texas Interscholastic League of Colored Schools (TILCS).

Coach Patterson was a no-nonsense coach who stressed fundamentals and a high degree of conditioning. One of the philosophies he lived by and often quoted was "A good big man could beat a good little man any time." He was constantly looking for players who had size, foot speed, heart, dedication, "smarts", and a willingness to work hard and think when playing sports. He would often tell his players that if they did not attend class or if they made poor grades, there was no place on his team for them.

He stressed academic achievement as being equally important as athletic performance.

On this particular day, after sending in the play, Coach Patterson leaned forward with both hands on his knees. He then pulled at his cap as if he were saluting and acknowledging his assistant coaches on the sideline. The Wheatley players dug in deeper as the Lions broke their huddle. As the Yates players approached the line of scrimmage, almost everyone in the place was puzzled by the formation. What play would they run? This formation was very strange as it resembled that for an extra point try. Ivory "Lumbunie" Jones, the starting guard, lined up in the backfield, and Wheat, the quarterback, was kneeling on the ground. What were they trying to do? The Wheatley players would not be fooled by this maneuver. The crowd of 30,000 plus was on its feet wondering, "What had Coach Patterson come up with now?"

Coach Patterson was known to be an innovative, very imaginative and creative coach. Many said he was well ahead of his time. On several occasions Coach Patterson would employ schemes and plays not seen by most coaches. The element of surprise, doing something out of the ordinary, bringing some unexpected element to the situation was his calling card. It was his trademark, his coaching style as he employed this keen sense of the unexpected. Bud Johnson, a local reporter for *The Informer,* said, "Patterson was not only a genius but a magician" (December 19, 1964). He continued, "Game after game, stunned fans watched as Pat, the magician, worked his magic and won again." One sports writer, when asked about Patterson's uncanny ability remarked, "How fantastic that man gets breaks." Coach Alexander Durley, a well known collegiate coach in the area, replied when asked about Patterson's breaks, "You make your breaks by exploiting every opportunity. This is just what Patterson did, exploited every opportunity" (December 19, 1964).

Andrew Pat Patterson was affectionately known by his players as the Hick or Hickman. All of the coaches had nicknames that the players used in secret to refer to them. Never, never, never would this nickname be used in public or in the presence of any adult, only in the circle of other players or students. Where did the name Hickman come from? Erroneous rumors had circulated that he was called the Hickman/Hick because of this funny little knot on the back of his head. Some said they called him that because he was from some small town back in the sticks of Illinois. Some individuals indicated that there was a college coach of some renown, innovative and well-respected with a reputation for calling trick plays which often worked against an opponent. His name was Herman Hickman, the head coach at Yale University.

Hickman was recognized as one of the most outstanding collegiate players of his era when he played linebacker for the Tennessee Volunteers. He went on to become an assistant coach at several major universities and was an outstanding coach of many famous all-star teams. He left the coaching ranks early and became well-known for his radio and TV commentary. One critic reported that his wit, humor, and great memory gained him a renowned reputation as a great banquet speaker and enabled him to become a national radio and television personality. One story concerning his reputation as a coach was told by Robin Hardin, who said, "Hickman had made his reputation as a defensive coach, and his tactical designs on offense often gave the impression of improvisation" (Wikipedia.org).

Several players from Patterson's 1951 squad, including Eugene Floyd, Edward "Bo" Murray, Ray Herman Jones, Robert McGowan, George Gray, and Robert Terry recalled that once they were practicing before an important district game and Coach Patterson had them running a series of new plays and formations. They were talking and asking one another, "What is he going to come up with next? He must think he is the Hickman or somebody." That is how the nickname came about, and the name stuck.

Waiting for the play, most Lion fans were puzzled. However, they knew from past experience that the coach would come up with something unusual. The Wildcat fans were confident that their team would stop the play whatever it was. "Field goal!" a few knowledgeable sports fans in small recesses of the stadium were saying. "Field goal! What is that?" some fans asked. They were soon to find out. The ball was snapped; it wobbled to Wheat, who set it down on the 13-yard line. Lumbunie, who had missed the extra point try earlier, approached the ball from the right hash marks, took one step, then two, brought the right leg forward and kicked the ball. The ball soared 23 yards and split the uprights. It's a score, three points for the mighty Jack Yates Lions! The Yates fans and supporters were in a state of wild delirium as they could not believe what they had just witnessed. The Wheatley fans were in utter disbelief. No high school player could kick a ball like that. In many instances they had found it difficult to kick an extra point after a touchdown from the two-yard line. To kick a 23-yard field gold was impossible. No way, utterly impossible.

A field goal! High school football players do not try for field goals, do they? Almost 16 years earlier, in 1938, in this same classic battle, Wheatley defeated Yates by a score of 9 to 6 as reported by Sam McKibben of *The Houston Informer* (December 3, 1938). He wrote that as time was about to expire in the fourth quarter, Yates had the ball on Wheatley's five-yard line. Yates ran three line plays for one yard each only to be repelled by the Wildcats. Earlier in the contest Wheatley had scored on a safety making the score 2-0. They then scored a touchdown and point after, giving them nine points. Yates had scored its only points late in the second period. Late in the fourth quarter Yates had a chance to tie the game. With the ball resting on the four-yard line, it was fourth and goal. A field goal would tie the score, but the attempt sailed wide, and Wheatley held on to win the game.

How ironic! A field goal would be the major factor in deciding the contest. Many a fan had seldom witnessed a field goal attempt in a schoolboy game. A few fans may have seen this maneuver executed by collegiate or professional players, but hardly ever by schoolboys. However, this day was to be the day for the golden Lions. The field goal try was good, and it put Yates ahead 9 to7 in the second quarter. This was the momentum the Lions needed to push ahead of the Wildcats.

Wheatley's next possession placed them deep in their own territory, and their failure to score resulted in the score's remaining 9 to 7 at the end of the first half. In the third period Wheatley scored a touchdown to go ahead 14-9. It was their last score of the afternoon. Late in the fourth quarter Yates mounted a come from behind drive and scored its last touchdown to go ahead 15 to 14. The game ended with Yates once again the victors. What a glorious day! What a glorious afternoon for the Lions' crimson and gold. The victory was sweet. Once again the boys from Third Ward had bragging rights for another year as the best Black high school team in the City of Houston.

Frank Walker

Frank Walker was reared in the Fifth Ward, where he attended Phillis Wheatley High School from 1934-36. He played in his first Yates-Wheatley contest in 1935. Walker said, "One of the biggest honors a Wheatley or Yates football player could have is to be able to play in The Game, and the Wheatley-Yates fiasco, with its excitement and tradition, will last a lifetime in reminiscences" (Informer November 26, 1966).

Upon graduation he was recruited by and played for Coach Ace Mumford at Southern University in Baton Rouge, Louisiana, where he made All-Conference at quarterback in 1937-38. While at Southern, Coach Walker also competed in track and field. After graduation in 1942, he served in WWII for four years. While in the army, Coach Walker made a promise that he always kept. He said, "Being at home on Thanksgiving Day for this game had made such an impression on me that I said once I got out of the Army, I would always be here for that day".

Returning home after serving in the army, Coach Walker began his coaching career by working a couple of years at Texas Southern University, a year at Southern University Laboratory School, and two years at E. O. Smith Jr. High School. He then went to Wheatley as an assistant coach in football and baseball. He served under Coach Countee before he became the head coach and retired as such in 1971. As head coach of the Wildcats, his team garnered the District and State Championships in 1954. He again won the District title in 1959.

Many of his players received college scholarships during his tenure, including Cyrus Lancaster, Aaron Jackson, Johnnie Gant, Gilbert Dixon, Donnie Davis, George Balthazar, Charles Williams, Herbert Broussard, Richard Holloway, Donald Ashley, and Godwin Turk. During his coaching career he was credited with being one of the most successful coaches in Texas. One of his coaching peers, Jackie Carr, said Franks' teams consistently were in position to win their district title as he never lost more than three games a year in his 17 years as head coach.

Chapter 4

FUN AND GAMES

**The world is round, and the place which
may seem like the end may also be only the
beginning.**
—Ivy Baker—

In the Lion's Den

It is now Wednesday. For several days alumni of both schools as well as other former residents have been arriving in anticipation of the exciting activities surrounding The Classic. As for the students, learning has been suspended—everything is in limbo until the big pep rally begins. Typical is the scene at Jack Yates High School.

"Give me an L! Give me an I! Give me an O! Give me an N! What's that spell?! LION! Fight! Fight! Fight!"

This was just one of the many yells and chants repeated over and over again at the pep rally. With great anticipation, expectations, and high excitement the students had looked forward to the big pep rally all week long. It was Wednesday afternoon during the fifth and sixth periods, and at that time all hell broke loose. It was impossible to curb the enthusiasm of the students as they packed the auditorium to yell and scream their heads off for the upcoming game on tomorrow. The Yates Lions were going to play the mighty Wildcats of Wheatley in the annual Turkey Day Classic. Wheatley had a perfect 9 and 0 season record at this point, and Yates had a 6 and 3 record. The season records had to be disregarded because anything was possible when these two rivals met on Thanksgiving Day. The Lions were determined to win this epic battle, no matter what, and so were the Wildcats. Bragging rights had to be extended another year as the Lions had whipped the Wildcats last year. But, before the battle it was pump-up time. It didn't take much to pump up spirits as everyone was eager and ready.

The auditorium was full, not an empty seat to be found. But who wanted to sit? No one! Students were standing around the auditorium walls. It seemed as if the entire student body was in this place. The auditorium would accommodate only about 600 students; therefore, there had to be two pep rallies to let everyone in on the action.

The famous marching band now sitting on the stage struck up one of Sousa's marches, and the cheerleaders jumped and cheered to the beat of the music. A party atmosphere was in the place. School pennants, posters and banners and flags were waving in the air as the band played on. At the completion of one tune, the cheerleaders would begin another chant. While everyone was chanting, the captain of the band kept an eye on the side door leading to the stage. When he spotted the football team players entering the side door to the stage, he would cue the band to strike up the tune "Hail, Hail, the Gangs all Here," immediately.

"Hail, Hail the gangs all here. What in the world do we care! What in the world do we care! Hail, Hail! The gangs all here, What in the world do we care now? Jack Yates gonna shine tonight, Jack Yates gonna shine. Jack Yates gonna shine tonight

Jack Yates gonna shine. Jack Yates gonna shine tonight, Jack Yates gonna shine. The Moon's gonna shine, Yates gonna shine,

Jack Yates gonna shine."

By this time the students' voices and enthusiasm were at fever pitch as the football team assembled on the stage in front of the band. Everybody was whooping it up, giving high fives, back slaps, and the victory sign.

About this time the captain of the cheering squad came to the microphone and asked the coaches to speak. Head coach Patterson addressed the audience and again emphasized the importance of the next day's contest. He emphasized both team's season records and indicated that the winner would have bragging rights for another year. Wheatley had already won the district title as it was undefeated this year. But, he stressed, our boys had something to prove—pride, tradition, and status as the best team in the city. With that said, he introduced the captains of the team, the starting line-up, and then the rest of the players, the team managers and trainers. Asking the students for their loyal support, he said the team needed it, reminding us that Wheatley's team also was proud of its record, its tradition and that they would be doing everything to defeat us on tomorrow. The team captains then spoke and asked the student body to cheer loud and be proud to be a Lion. As the captains spoke, it was hard to hear exactly what was said, as the student body was restless and wanted to shout and cheer even more.

Pep rallies were a time to let one's hair down, time to let loose, time to show one's school spirit. However, the Thanksgiving pep rally was special because of the impending holiday and the cross-town rivals. Both schools were fiercely loyal, and the magnitude of what was to happen the next day made it significantly important to all students. As the band continued to play and the cheerleaders led their favorite chants, everyone had a wonderful time.

The Cat's Breakfast Feast

It is now Thursday—THE DAY! Wheatley alumni and ex-students began the day's celebration with a 7:00 a.m. Thanksgiving breakfast celebration in the school's cafeteria. While many alumni and ex students attended the breakfast, hundreds more were assembling in front of the school awaiting the start of the Wildcat's parade. Initiated in 1950 according to newspaper accounts, the breakfast became so popular it continued yearly through 1966. The special feature of the celebration was the crowning of Miss Alumna. Each year local radio station KCOH broadcast one hour of the event with Clifton "King Bee" Smith as its live host. Besides cheers and pep chants, and a lot of "whooping it up", guest appearances of famous alumni was anticipated and highlighted the breakfast.

As one entered into the cafeteria the sight of purple and white decorations were hung beautifully throughout the room. All of the walls were covered with the Wheatley pennants, banners and posters, and the dining tables were covered with purple and white tablecloths. The aroma of freshly cooked eggs, grits, crispy bacon, and hot buttered biscuits filled the nostrils. Hot coffee and tea along with sweet rolls were available for all. The atmosphere was lively, boisterous, full of high spirits and merriment. Dignitaries were seated in-front-of, and on a raised podium including, Miss Alumna and her escort, the school's principal, and community leaders. A dish jockey was positioned to one side of the podium, and provided recorded music throughout the morning. The music was lively, upbeat and loud as it too filled the room. The people were energized by the music as they clapped their hands and patted their feet to the rhythmic beat. Many of the students and some alumni had difficulty staying in their seats, fighting the urge to dance in the isles between the tables. Although it was early morning school spirits were high and began to overflow throughout the room. The festive gathering provided those in attendance with the opportunity to release pent-up emotions, to cheer loud and long, and to boast of their school's football accomplishments. Aside from the lively spirited cheers and intermingling yells the main occasion called for remarks by the school's principal, alumni president, Miss Alumna, and the student body president.

After introductory remarks and the subsidence of the spirited yells and chants everyone lined-up for the breakfast feast. There were a few eager beavers who scrambled to be first in line, but the majority of those in attendance were orderly and courteous. Once served the guest took their seats and consumed the scrumptious meal. The food was hot, delicious, and "finger licking good". While the meal was being consumed small talk about the afternoon game could be heard throughout the room. One ardent and faithful supporter was overheard as he spoke softly to several friends around him, saying, "It's no way the Lions can beat us this year. We have the best quarterback in the state and our defense has allowed the fewest points of any team in the district." "You know," he continued, "we should have won that game last year. Fumbling the ball into the endzone with less than a minute to play, and Yates recovering the ball cost us that game. This year will be different, we'll take this one."

Near the end of the breakfast several more yells and chants brought the crowd to a fever's pitch. The room was bursting with excitement as all yelled in unison Wheatley! Wheatley! Wheatley! A few additional remarks were given as the breakfast came to a close. The enthusiastic alumni and students were ready for the ballgame as they departed.

Attending the Thanksgiving breakfast feast meant one had to rise early, make ones way to the school's cafeteria, meet and greet friends and alumni, and cheer, yell, and make a lot of noise in support of the mighty Wildcats. Surely when the breakfast ended ones' nutritional needs were met, as-well-as ones' emotional zeal heighten.

A Band Members Anticipated Joy
(As described by a Yates band member of the 1950s)

Crowds begin assembling early to secure a good spot from which to watch the "send offs" for the big day—the Wheatley High School parade winding through the Fifth Ward and the Jack Yates High School parade marching down Third Wards' "Main Street": This student describes his participation in the Third Ward event—from early morning eager anticipation through the march to its culmination at Yates High School.

Weeks and days before Thanksgiving my thoughts centered on the Thanksgiving football game and the annual parade down Dowling Street. Excitement, enthusiasm and anxiety filled my thoughts each day and the pep rally at school on Wednesday heightened my emotions. In just a few hours we would be marching down Dowling with hundred of Yates fans yelling, shouting and cheering us on.

Last night and early this morning I could hardly sleep. I was up very early, anticipating the parade which would occur in a few hours. It was not unlike the four previous Thanksgiving mornings that I could recall as a band member of the Mighty Lion's band. Mr. Will Henry Bennett, band director, had informed us that we were to meet him at 8:00 a.m. on the corner of Dowling and Gray, the starting point of the parade. He had emphasized, "Do not be late." Mr. Bennett did not play around. If he told you not to be late, he meant it. If you were late you were in serious trouble, and you might not march in the parade. Mr. Bennett, whom the students all affectionately called "Prof", was a middle-aged man somewhat slightly built, about 5'9", with a light brown complexion and mingled gray hair. He had a broad nose and a warm smile and personality. His voice was soft, and his language was always precise. "Prof" was a superb musician, well known for his musical talent.

Wheatley's band director, Samuel Harris, and Washington's band director, Conrad Johnson, were also well-known for the talented musicians they had produced throughout the years. The three directors were also renowned not only in the Black community of Houston, but throughout the State of Texas. They were well-versed in all forms of music from that of marching bands, symphony and concert bands, to that of jazz combos and orchestras. They themselves could perform all types of music. When it came to performing in parades and half-time shows at football games, their bands were truly outstanding.

My sister and I lived in the South Union/Sunnyside community, which was about five miles south of Third Ward. To be on time for the parade meant that someone had to drive us to the parade site. The city busses did not run early in the Black community, and the Black-owned Pioneer busses' schedule began even later in the day. Each of the four previous years my Dad had taken us to the site of the parade.

My sister was one of the officers in the Ryan Kadettes, the famous girls' drill team of 100 members plus. They did precision drills and had any number of intricate formations. These girls could "strut their stuff" with precision drills in their military-looking uniforms of red skirts and gold jackets, white boots, white gloves and white plumes on their red and gold trimmed hats. It made for an impressive sight. My sister was second in command of this year's squad. Mrs. Bonnie Branch Holland was the sponsor and had been such for many years.

As we left the house, my Dad asked, "Do you have everything?" "Yes", I answered. Many times in a hurry to get some place I would forget something, and this was not one of the times to forget my instrument or mouthpiece. The weather was unseasonably warm for late November. However, I was somewhat cold-natured; so the weather suited me. As we drove the five miles to Third Ward, there was little conversation among the three of us. I recall my dad's asking what time we thought the parade would end and where he should pick us up. I said, "Oh, we should be finished around 10:30 or so, and pick us up in front of the school on Elgin." He said, "Okay."

Dad continued, "Who's going to win the game today?" I replied, "We will," as I began to tell him what kind of team we had and what our record was as opposed to Wheatley's season record. But, more often than not, season records had absolutely nothing to do with this game. Both teams would be 'sky high', and anything could happen. But, being a loyal Lion, I was more than confident that we would win the game. "Well", he said, "we'll see, won't we?" We pulled up to the corner of Dowling and Gray about 7:35 a.m. Dad let us out of the car and said he would see us in a little while. As he drove off, I thought to myself, "He does this every year, never complains, and picks us up after the parade is over. Oh, well, that's a good dad for you."

A Lion's Strut

The Yates parade route began at the corner of Dowling and Gray in the heart of Third Ward. Dowling Street flowed north and south, and was the main street in the community. It was also one of the busiest streets as many business establishments lined both sides of the street for more than a mile. Gray Street was a cross street flowing east and west, which had a small number of businesses located on it. Located on Gray Street one block west of Dowling was St. John Baptist Church, one of the major Black churches in Houston with a large congregation. Before the parade began, some of the marching units were lined up in front of the church, while other units were east of Dowling on Gray. The parade Marshall stood at the corner of Dowling and Gray waving her hands high in the air directing units to fall into the procession. The mighty Lion's band lined up east of Dowling on Gray, and led all units in the parade. The excitement mounted as the band struck up one of its favorite tunes. No sooner had the parade begun to march, it immediately turned south on Dowling Street. The other marching units began filling in behind the band at the parade Marshall's signal. The crowds that had assembled were lively and in great spirits. As the band boomed its music Dowling Street became alive. The parade marched past the Dowling Theater located on the west side of the street as large groups of school-age children and their parents lined the street. Adjacent to the Dowling Theater were a number of stores, including a variety store, drug store and a dress shop. Directly across the street from the theater on the east side was a furniture store, a bed and mattress store, and Rollins Jewelry.

The next cross street after Gray was Webster Street, where Wesley Chapel AME Church was located. Wesley Chapel was one of the largest Black Methodist churches in Houston. It too boasted a membership well into the thousands. On the opposite side of the street stood the Atlanta Life building. There was also a physician's office and a hamburger/ ice-cream restaurant next to the Atlanta Life building, and Rubenstein Clothiers, an upscale store for men. Spectators lining both sides of the street cheered and applauded enthusiastically as the parade passed.

Following the band were the Ryan Kadettes, the drum and bugle corps, cheerleaders, well decorated floats, and a number of automobiles carrying Miss Yates and her court, school social club officers, community dignitaries, and faculty and staff members. Those automobiles had to be the finest in the land. Big, bright, super El Dorado Cadillacs, Buicks, and Oldsmobiles, with their long hoods, white-walled tires and back fender skirts were positioned precisely for their impressive presentation. Each vehicle was "clean to the bone", its shine mirror bright. Those cars were so fine you would give your lunch money just to ride in one.

A festive event it was as everyone became engulfed in the merriment of the moment. The band continued to played from a repertoire of John Phillip Sousa's marches, including *Washington Post, The Thunderer, Semper Fidelis, National Emblem, El Capitan and King Cotton*. One of the band's favorite Sousa's marches was *Them Bases*. It highlighted the bass instruments. This piece of music had significant passages throughout which featured the trombone, baritone and bass horns. One could feel the pulsating beat, the oscillating twinge and the roaring of these bass instruments, playing in rhythm highlighted by the beat of the big bass drum.

Leading the parade down Dowling Street, the majorettes were "strutting their stuff," high-stepping, prancing and dancing to the rhythms of the music and tempo of the drum beats. The crowds grew larger as the parade passed the Senate, a popular night club, and the Ajapo Hotel just north of McGowan, another cross street. The Ajapo was one of two hotels in the Third Ward community which housed guests from out-of-town. Major hotels in Houston like the Shamrock Hilton and the Lamar Fleming Hotels did not allow Black guests. Directly across the street from The Senate were the Lone Star Barbershop and the Grand Court Order of Calanthe building, and next to it was an optometrist's entomologist office and Texas State Optical. As the Jack Yates parade continued along Dowling, past McGowan Street, there was a gasoline station on the corner and Wolf's department store next to it. Directly across the street from the gasoline stations were a family restaurant, another night spot and clothes cleaning business. Next to the cleaning business was the original St. John's Baptist Church boasting the largest Black congregation in Houston, with well over 5,000 members. There were a number of other establishments on the west side of Dowling, south of the church including a rooming house, Standard Make Shoe Store for men, and another drug store. Across the street from these establishments were the Emancipation Park Movie Theater and the Square Deal Taxi Cab Company. The crowds grew larger in numbers once the parade neared Square Deal Taxi Cab Company. Rettigs Ice Cream Parlor faced the Emancipation Park which was bounded on the north by Tuam Street and on the south by Elgin Street. There seemed to be several hundred more people in Emancipation Park as the parade passed. Emancipation Park was the first public park in Houston. The park land was originally purchased by several Black citizens including the late John Henry Jack Yates. The band was in full swing as they began to play a popular rock and roll tune of the late 1950s. People began dancing in the streets and singing along with the band as the beat of the music energized them. Not only were the adults having a wonderful time, but the children who lined the streets also got in on the action. Those assembled along the parade route held up pennants and banners and waved then in the air shouting and clapping and yelling all at the same time. It was easy to tell these folk loved the parade. Deafening were the sounds; pulsating and exciting were the rhythms as music filled the air. Dancing in the streets, party time, it was a rocking rolling good time for everyone. This was what enlivened the community, giving rise to the festive atmosphere which would have carry over to that of the afternoon football game. There were hundreds of well-wishers clapping their hands and patting their feet; it seemed the entire community was present and involved.

As the parade proceeded along its route, the musicians became drenched in perspiration on this warm November day. The excitement of it all, the enthusiasms of the spectators made their efforts seem tireless. Band members were too caught up in the excitement of the moment and the anticipation of the afternoon game such that their energy levels were heightened rather than depleted. As the parade participants passed Emancipation Park and a host of other business establishments they turned off Dowling and headed east on Elgin Street toward the school, where the parade ended.

The parade participants disassembled and members went in several directions from the school building. One excited band member could be heard above the bustling crowd saying, "We can't be stopped now! Bring on those Wildcats," as he put away his instrument before heading home.

While the Yates parade proceeded, simultaneously across town the Wheatley Wildcats parade was being held. Their parade route proceeded along Market Street beginning at Wheatley High School, to Waco Street, then Lyons Avenue to Lockwood and back to the school. Witnesses indicated the music was loud but festive and that spectators lined both sides of the streets. Most of the individuals observing the parade were in a holiday mood and enjoyed the activities. The parade was led by the school band conducted by Sammie Harris, followed by the purple and white squadron under the leadership of Dicie G. Cleveland. The squadron was followed by the most beautifully decorated floats and automobiles in Houston carrying the school's queen and her court, Miss Alumni, campus club officers, and other community dignitaries.

Inasmuch as Wheatley and Yates High Schools each held separate parades in their respective communities the morning of the big football game that afternoon both communities were enlivened. The communities were geared up and looked forward with eager anticipation to the jubilant celebration. The parades and all of the other activities surrounding the football contest were the highlight of the Thanksgiving holiday.

Chelsie Banks, a correspondent for *The Houston Informer* (1966) wrote about the last Thanksgiving parade. She reported that this was one of the most spectacular parades ever staged in Texas' scholastic history. Continuing she said, "The parades spark the fire of enthusiasm for the game, which follows." Reporting on the impact of not having a parade or game on Thanksgiving Day also meant that other events and activities affiliated with the Classic would also be lost. "Further," she continued, "the Classic has been called the largest regularly scheduled high school football game in the nation." An additional article appearing in the Sports Section of *The Houston Informer* (12/1/56) also indicated the annual football game between the two schools had grown to be the nation's number one game with regards to attendance. The attendance at the 1955 game, as reported by stadium officials, was over 31,000. The article went on to report, "The nearest public school football games, drawing such a crowd is in Chicago, played between a public school team and a Catholic school team, and it is not a yearly affair."

In Houston year in and year out the parades were a living, breathing, emotional, gathering of participants and community supporters, families and friends of the respective schools. These parades had tradition and were expected to give spirit to the students, past, present and future, and to the many followers of both the Third and Fifth Ward communities.

Get Your Ducketts Early

Game time!! Tickets for the Thanksgiving Day game had been on sale weeks in advance, available at numerous businesses in the Black communities. The Public School Stadium had only four ticket windows on the east and west sides of the stadium on the day of the game. Those who failed to purchase their tickets early would have to wait in very long lines the day of the game. A very conservative estimate of those who regularly attended the Classic was 20,000. Imagine 20,000 plus individuals trying to purchase tickets at these eight ticket windows during the day of the game. Most folk knew what a hassle it would be like to stand in long lines on the day of the game to get tickets, therefore many followed the advice of local officials and purchased their tickets prior to the day of the game.

Each year the attendance was such that the seating capacity of the stadium was insufficient to accommodate the number of fans desiring to attend, and standing room space was also scarce. Those who failed to purchase presale tickets had to stand and wait in extremely long lines, which stretched for more than a city block at each ticket window.

J. Carr, a loyal, Wheatley alumnus, told this story. "It was my custom to get to the game early to avoid having to stand in long lines for tickets. The gates opened at 12:00 noon, but I always got there around 11:00 a.m. If you wanted a seat in the stadium, and didn't already have a ticket you had to follow this pattern. I had an aunt visiting from California one Thanksgiving who had heard about the game for many years. She insisted that I take her to the game. Well, I really didn't want to, but I eventually agreed. It took her so long to get dressed that by the time we left Fifth Ward it was well past 12:00 noon. We rode the city bus, which dropped us off at the corner of Holman and Scott Streets. There were people in lines to purchase tickets from Scott Street to the stadium. By the time we purchased tickets and got in the stadium it was halftime". End of the story.

Chapter 5

DRESSED TO KILL

People are like stained-glass windows. They sparkle and shine when the sun is out, but when the darkness sets in, their beauty is revealed only if there is a light from within.
—Elizabeth Kubler Ross—

All who planned to attend the Turkey Day Classic wanted a new outfit to wear or presumed one was needed. It had become a long standing tradition to dress up in one's finest attire because everyone else would be adhering to this tradition. One's finest attire meant "sprucing up" in order to see and be seen. Most did not spare expense when it came to this occasion. One's best go-to-meeting attire and Sunday best was the order of the day. A complete outfit was the requirement or whatever made you look good in one's own eyes.

Two alumnae were talking about the Classic and what they planned to wear to the game. One asked, "What are you going to wear tomorrow?"

"Girl", answered her friend, "I got this outfit months ago. I can hardly wait to put it on. It's got this and that, and the coat to match is a knockout."

Home girl replied, "That suit seems a bit heavy for this weather. You're going to burn up tomorrow if you wear that."

"Look!" was the reply, "It could be 90 degrees out there tomorrow, and I'm wearing this bad boy. This thing fits me so fine that I know I'm going to knock them dead. Last year I got so many compliments that I had to do myself one better. When those guys see me with this on, I'll have to fight them off with a cane."

Shopping and dressing for the Thanksgiving game was an annual obligation, a matter of personal pride that almost everyone looked forward to. Nothing but one's very best would do. Last year's outfit would not do. The men, women and children had to have new outfits, from head to toe: shoes, hats, gloves, topcoat, jewelry and furs. For months in advance nearly everyone who planned to attend the game began shopping for outfits to wear. These outfits were also for the after-game parties.

What about the cost of such goods? The cost did not matter. Some people would save for this special event; others would place their items "on lay-away" at department stores and pay a small amount each week until the items were paid for. Lay-away was a very popular payment plan "back in the day". Most people did not have a lot of cash on hand, nor were they making great wages, nor were there credit cards available; therefore, this method of payment for goods was very popular and convenient. The merchants would hold your goods at their establishments until the cost was paid in full.

How long would the lay-away last? It depended on the amount of the sale and the amount you could afford to pay each week. A best guess would be that it would take five to six months of equal payments to pay in full. Local merchants did not worry about customers' not paying off the lay-away accounts, because they knew that this was a very special event in the Black community and that the overwhelming majority of those who used this payment plan would make good on their accounts. Moreover, if a customer defaulted on an account, the merchant could restock the goods and place them on sale at a later date. It was a "win-win" situation for the merchants.

During the 1920s thru the 1950s there were no shopping malls in Houston, and most of the clothing stores were centered in downtown Houston. However, there were some small, but prestigious tailor shops in the Black communities which also did "turn away" business during this time.

Some of the merchants selling clothing during this era included Foley's, Rubenstein's, Woolworth's, Bonds Clothiers, Palais Royal, Sakowitz, Battlestein's, Mocks, Isabelle Gerhart, Zindler's Clothiers, and Krupp and Tuffly's, which were all located in downtown Houston. Third Ward and Fifth Ward neighborhood shops included Pleas Smith Tailors, Burton Tailors, Caldwell Tailors, Best Tailors, and Standard Make Shoes.

The men's outfits included sport jackets or suits, and a wide necktie with formal print design was deemed appropriate. Many outfits came with bright colored suspenders for the slacks. A hat, one with a wide brim was preferred by most. Alligator shoes were top of the line if one could afford them, and sometimes spats would be added. A long dangling gold chain was also popular at the time. A jazzy top coat would be worn or draped over the left arm if the weather was too warm for one to wear it. Leather gloves topped off "the look". Because spectators had to cross the dusty parking lots before entering the stadium, the shoeshine boys outside the stadium did "turn-away" business as many men wanted their shoes to have a high gloss finish when they entered the stadium.

The women were not to be outdone by the men when it came to displaying their garments. During this period there were no pant suits for women, therefore the dresses and suits came in an assortment of designs and styles. Most of the dresses and skirts were knee length or longer. Most accentuated the curves and shapes of the female figure. A silk blouse or designer sweater might also be worn. The mink or fur coat was appropriate and worn by those who could afford such. A "dazzy hat" adorned the head which allowed that beautiful recent hairdo to be seen. Silk stockings were required, and high heel shoes which matched the outfit were in order. A small purse and hand gloves to match the shoes were required.

The majority of fans in attendance "sported "the finest outfits. They resembled a parade of stars. "Oohs" and "Ahs" could be heard throughout the stadium. The long stares, heads bobbing up and down, and raised eyebrows indicated onlookers approved of the fashions on parade. Heads would turn left and then right as this scene played itself out all afternoon. However, being "sharp" and "dressed-to-kill" did not prohibit fans from shouting and cheering for their favorite team. The festive attire enlivened the atmosphere of this gala event making it a 'happening'.

The thousands of fans seated on both sides of the stadium as well as those standing around the playing field had come to witness and be a part of the festive annual event. They had come dressed in their best attire to see and be seen. The weather conditions did not matter, for this was a onetime yearly affair. The nature of the activity, the greeting of friends old and new made for many the opportunity to catch or be caught. This scene repeated itself all afternoon as fans were decked out in their very best "Dressed to Kill".

Chapter 6

A THREE RING CIRCUS

Don't be content with average because average is just as close to the bottom as it is to the top.
—Danielle Ballentine—

Halftime of the Classic was like watching a Three Ring Circus, with many things happening at the same time. Ones' attention was directed toward watching the drill squads and marching bands, the fancy automobiles and decorative floats with the school's queen, and the sea of "dressed to kill" fans. The marching bands and other performing groups began to head for the field five minutes before half-time. Getting to the field was a chore in and of itself as thousands of fans were along the sidelines and end zones. Every year there were so many people attending the game that every seat in the stadium was taken. The overflow crowd lined the playing field four or five deep so that there were literally thousands of fans to navigate through for the performing groups to get onto the field. The police and extra security guards had to assist the performing groups in taking their places in order to take the field. Lining up and falling into formation became a real challenge for those who were performing. Wheatley's contingents were lined up on the north end of the field, and Yates' performers were lined up at the opposite end of the field.

Wheatley's band director, Samuel D. Harris, was excited, but also disturbed as he tried to maneuver his group through the large crowd of fans, into its proper position so that they might take the field in less than three minutes. The game was still in progress with the score tied at seven apiece and the Wheatley team in possession of the ball at mid-field. It was third down and eight as the Wheatley quarterback retreated and threw a long pass down field toward the goal line, but the ball fell incomplete at the 15-yard line. It was now fourth down, and Wheatley had to punt.

The ball was snapped to the punter, who got off a booming, high end-over-end kick. The ball landed at the four-yard line, took a high bounce over the head of the Yates player and out of the end zone literally into the Wheatley band, which was lined up to take the field. The band members scampered and fell back, giggling, jumping around, pushing one another in an effort to dodge the wayward ball. It was all in fun as the official retrieved the ball and proceeded to run back up field to spot it at the 20-yard line. The band members began reassembling in formation as there was now less than a minute before halftime. Time for one or two plays and surely Yates would not try anything fancy 80 yards away from pay dirt. On first down the ball was lateraled to the fullback, who plunged into the line of scrimmage for no gain. On second down the same play netted two yards. As the teams unpiled, they looked up at the clock to find time had expired. Both teams on the field and the players and coaches on the sidelines headed for the dressing rooms at the south end of the stadium. A pathway had to be cleared for the teams to exit the field and pass thru the spectators.

It was now halftime and the school which was designated as the visitors would take the field first. The schools would alternate as the home team or visiting team each year throughout the duration of the Classic. Wheatley was designated as the visiting school this year and their performing units took the field led by their band. Majorettes began to prance and high step their way onto the field. The band members began their march, playing their music, desperately trying to keep their lines straight and keep in step. Spectators were paying close attention as they looked to see whether or not the band lines were straight, and if they were not, whistles and cat calls could be heard throughout the stands.

While the band, purple and white squadron, brigadiers and other performing groups were on the field, the shinny vehicles and floats stationed on the north end of the field, began to start their motors to enter the stadium and drive around the oval track which surrounded the football field. The track was composed of fine cinder fragments, and when the automobiles passed over it, dust began to rise. Those shinny automobiles sparkling earlier in the afternoon sun were being coated with a fine mist of red dust. The dust was no problem as alumni viewed these processions. This was a proud moment for the school. As the automobiles and floats circled the track, the queen and her court would wave to the onlookers who were smiling and enjoying the festive moment. After circling the track the vehicles and floats stopped at the 50-yard line to allow the queen and her entire entourage to depart and be escorted to the center of the playing field. As the queen walked to the center of the field she turned and faced her home stands, to be crowned and presented flowers by the school's principal and his staff. Each school worked very hard to outshine the other in presenting its school's queen and her court. Which school had the best looking, most prestigious brand of automobiles? Which school had the best designed and decorated floats?

This was a yearly ritual, and both schools took pride in presenting its queen. It was a real show stopper. The queen and her court were dressed in the best attire available from head to toe. Glitter and "bling" adorned their garments. "Dressed to the finest" was how most fans would describe this occasion. What a glorious moment! What a beautiful spectacle! The crowd was in awe at the sight of this beautiful pageantry. Fans were quiet; there was little to no movement in the stands as everyone's eyes were fixed on the ceremony. The band assembled in the background played soft melodies which stirred the heart. The photographers were busy taking photos—*flash, flash, flash*-of the momentous occasion. As the roses and flowers were presented to the queen and her court, the tiara placed on the queen's head, the band ended its soft music to play the school's alma mater.

Upon completion of the ceremonies the entourage returned to their vehicles, and the opposing school then presented its queen. The competition between schools was more than an athletic one, as each school tried to outdo the other with the presentation of its queen. In 1958 Yates fans and supporters proudly proclaimed they were clearly the victors of the halftime spectacle. As usual the automobiles circled the field and stopped at the 50-yard line. Everyone began to ask, "Where is Carolyn Wilkins, Miss Yates, and Her Court?" "Where are they?" an agitated fan shouted. "It's time for them to take the field. It's time for the queen and her court to be recognized. Let us admire her exquisite beauty and grace." There was a buzz in the stands as no one knew what was happening.

All of a sudden there was a faint noise high above the stadium, and a small object appeared in the sky. "What is that?" fans were shouting. All eyes were now turned skyward as a helicopter was seen descending closer and closer to the stadium. As it came nearer, it began to hover over the field. With its blades swirling and the gusting sound of a mighty wind, the whirly bird landed at the 50-yard line of the playing field and out stepped Miss Yates and her court. The Yates fans on the west side of the stadium went into hysteria. The Wheatley Fans on the east side of the stadium were stunned in utter disbelief. Mouths flew open, heads were shaking, and even a few groans were uttered. The Yates fans let out a roar so loud, so deafening that it shook the stadium's foundation. Surely this had to be a moment to be remembered. In the history of this game never had the crowds been awe struck as they were on this day. The pageantry and splendor of the presentation was something that would be talked about for years to come.

Halftime was surely a time to celebrate the occasion. All of the beauty, pageantry and elegance of the afternoon seemed to culminate with the halftime program. The queens and their courts, the bands, the drill squads, and the fancy automobiles, all helped to make the entire event a moment to remember, until next year.

Half-Time "Excursions"

The majority of the fans keep their seats for the halftime show. However, some would venture down stairs to the restrooms and concession stands. Those who did would be people watching as they went, but at the same time trying their best to complete their errands quickly so that they could hurry back to catch some of the remaining halftime entertainment. Completing either task was quite a challenge. The restrooms had lines and lines of people waiting to get in. Many women and girls were escorting and even carrying young children who were constantly reminding their elders of the urgency of their visit. To get to the concession stands with their inviting smell of fresh popcorn, peanuts and hot dogs was even more difficult. Little boys and girls were saying things like "I'm hungry" and "Mommy can I have something to drink?" Further delays occurred as people saw old acquaintances and made small talk concerning the weather, complimenting one another on their attire, and analyzing the game and offering their predictions of the outcome. Each year one might comment about the sea of individuals congregated in these congested areas and refer to this as a "happening". It was the place to be, to see and be seen.

In the stands were teenage boys and some young men with white aprons around their waists, a boat shaped white hat on their heads, and heavy containers loaded with cold drinks and food. They were doing their best to serve the fans refreshments so that the concession stands would not be overrun. Hawking their wares, they cried, "Peanuts, popcorn, cold drinks, get your peanuts, popcorn, cold drinks here!" Most of these concessionaires would not have to travel far before having to refill their containers and reload.

Leaving one's seat in the stadium for the restrooms or the concession stands at halftime was an adventure all its own. The sheer volume of people, the mixed aromas of individual fragrances and a variety of foods combined in crowded spaces could be overwhelming. This was the nature of things at halftime when one ventured into the concession areas of the stadium. There was never a quick return to one's seat or standing place as the sea of people moved about very slowly. However, it was the place to see and be seen. The halftime show took place both on and off the field.

Chapter 7

FROM BETTER TO BEST,
THE CLASSIC BECOMES A LEGEND

**To be upset over what you don't have
is to waste what you do have.
—Ken Keyes—**

The three Black high schools in Houston, Booker T. Washington of Fourth Ward, Phyllis Wheatley of Fifth Ward, and Jack Yates of Third Ward, played their first games in 1927 at old Barr's field located on Bonner St. and S.P. Track, just off Washington Avenue out near the Heights. A few games were played in West End Park built in 1905 and referred to as the Mecca of Houston sports, located at Andrews and Heiner, south of downtown. When Buffalo Stadium, a minor league baseball facility was constructed in 1928, the games were moved to that site until the construction of the Houston Public School Stadium in 1942, then all HISD football games moved to the newly built stadium.

When constructed the HISD Public School Stadium seating capacity was 20,500, which was well above the 12,000 seating capacity at Buffalo Stadium. The Public School Stadium was renamed Jeppesen Stadium by HISD's board in 1958, in honor of HISD's board trustee Holger Jeppesen, who vigorously lobbied for its construction. Local fans who regularly attended activities at the stadium affectionately referred to the stadium as Jepp. The stadium's seating capacity was temporarily increased to 36,000 in 1960, to accommodate the Houston Oilers professional football team. One columnist reported that Lamar High School played the first game in the new stadium September 11, 1942 where they defeated Dallas W. H. Adamson 27-7 before a crowd of 14,500.

Prior to HISD's building the Public School Stadium the largest number of fans in attendance at the Yates/ Wheatley game was estimated to be 18,000 at Buffalo Stadium. When the games moved to the Public School Stadium, it soon became clear to HISD administration that the Yates vs. Wheatley games on Thanksgiving Day were drawing the largest attendance; therefore this game became permanently scheduled for Thanksgiving Day. This meant there would be no more Wheatley vs. Washington or Yates vs. Washington games played on Thanksgiving Day.

The Stadium(s) and Elbowroom

Many stories have been reported concerning the numbers of fans in attendance at the Turkey Day Classic. During the early years at Barr's field, East End Park and Buffalo stadium before the game became a Thanksgiving Classic, attendance grew each year. One source indicated that about close to a thousand fans attended the first game at Barr's field during 1927. The style of play of the Black schools was somewhat different from that of their white counterparts. Yates, Wheatley and Washington teams employed a wide open offensive style of play with backs spinning, a wide variety of end runs and laterals, reverses, use of the forward pass, and their clever adaptation of the Notre Dame offensive style. This exciting brand of football intrigued the true sports fan, and many white fans attended these games. A newspaper article appearing in *The Houston Post Dispatch* (Nov. 27, 1930) reported, "A special section will be reserved for whites." This notation appeared each year in articles advertising the game. One *Post* reporter attributed the large attendance to the novelty of the occasion as well as the fact that the game would be played on a holiday.

Newspapers during the early 1930s would report attendance accounts as "a large crowd of fans", or "a large enthusiastic gathering of fans". For the 1935 game *The Informer* reported that 6.000 fans were in attendance. In 1937 *The Houston Post* reported a holiday crowd of approximately 8,000 football-mad fans in attendance, and the 1938 attendance figures were quite similar. In 1939 a crowd of 8,000 fans witnessed the contest played on a rain soaked muddy field.

Reports of exact attendance figures proved to be questionable sometimes. On many occasions the figures would reflect estimated attendance, whereas at other times the figures would be the actual paid attendance. *The Houston Post, Houston Chronicle* and *Houston Informer* reported figures which clearly indicated that attendance at the Black high school games was significantly greater than that at the white high schools. For example, for a 1940 game between Lamar and Reagan High Schools played the night before Thanksgiving the attendance reported was 2,600 fans. The Yates vs. Wheatley Thanksgiving Day game reportedly drew 9,000 fans.

In 1941 the attendance soared to 14,000 fans as Wheatley beat Yates 7-0. According to Jay Don Davis of *The Houston Informer,* the first Thanksgiving Day game to be played in the new HISD Public School Stadium in 1942 saw Yates defeat Wheatley 12-7 before an estimated crowd of 15, 000 fans. There were no attendance figures reported for the 1943 game. However, in 1944 a crowd of 18,000 was present for the Wheatley 6-0 win.

The 1945 game, played the Thursday after Thanksgiving, showed an attendance report of 8,000 as Yates throttled Wheatley 26-0. Yates played Booker T. Washington on Thanksgiving Day before a crowd of 13,000 fans to win 12-0 in a thrilling affair. In 1946 no attendance figures were available. In 1947 a near capacity crowd turned out to see Yates defeat Wheatley 12-6. A crowd of 17,500 fans witnessed a 0-0 score in 1948. The 1949 affair saw the attendance increase to 21,000 as Wheatley edged Yates 7-6 in a nailbiter. In 1950 Yates' 28-6 defeat of Wheatley took place before a holiday crowd of 20,000 plus. From 1951 to 1966, attendance at the Thanksgiving Day Classic continued to grow.

Date	Winner	Score	Attendance
1951	Yates	26-19	28,000
1952	Wheatley	12-0	23,000
1953	Yates	22-16	25,000
1954	Yates	15-14	31,000
1955	Tie	0-0	24,437
1956	Wheatley	21 18	22,221
1957	Yates	12-6	30,450
1958	Wheatley	20-8	22,000 (rain)
1959	Wheatley	28-0	22,283
1960	Wheatley	3-0	29,000
1961	Yates	21-15	40,000 plus
1962	Yates	32-12	37,000
1963	Yates	21-14	19,864 (rain)
1964	Yates	25-0	22,478
1965	Yates	7-6	26,000
1966	Yates	6-3	28,121 (final Classic)

From 1949 game attendance was reported to be 20,000 plus with one exception, a rain date in 1963 until the final Thanksgiving Day game in 1966.

The attendance figures quoted above were taken from newspaper accounts in *The Houston Post*, *The Houston Informer*, *The Houston Chronicle*, *The Forward Times* and *The Houston Press*. However, one local reporter, who had witnessed many Classics during the 1950s, indicated that for several years attendance figures were reported well below the actual numbers. He based his statement on the fact that Houston's professional football team, the Oilers had begun playing its home games in Jeppesen Stadium also on September 11, 1960. The reporter indicated that actual attendance figures for the Thanksgiving Classic had been withheld at the discretion of HISD officials and administrators because these figures were well above the stadiums' capacity in violation of city safety codes.

Chapter 8

ZEBRAS AND THEIR STRIPES:
GAME DAY

**When faced with a challenge, look for a way,
not a way out.
—David Weatherford—**

Having to officiate the "Turkey Day Classic", a game of such magnitude, called for special preparation, courage, attention to detail, and most of all, honesty, integrity and fairness. Imagine you are one of four whose responsibility is to be impartial to both teams while making judgment calls which could impact the final outcome of the game. Both Yates and Wheatley communities looked forward to this game each year. Tens of thousands of spectators would be eying every move and call you made and would scrutinize and second-guess you on many of them. Most of the officials lived in the Houston community and were well known by many of the parents, students and friends who attended the Classic.

When asked to recall which game was most memorable, one official replied, "The 1962 game". Many would agree; however, some would disagree and name other years. On the day of the game in 1962, the weather was unseasonably warm. The sky was baby-blue with a few puffy white clouds. The sun shone bright, and it was a most pleasant day. The temperature was in the low 70s, perfect for playing football.

Several hours prior to the game the officiating team assembled in the officials' dressing room around noon. The room was small with a few lockers, a couple of benches and a couple of folding chair. There was a two-man shower and one commode in the rear area. The walls were painted gray, and the floor had been freshly mopped as a light sent of ammonia filled the air.

After the officiating team assembled, the referee began covering the basic rules and individual responsibilities. He cautioned the men to pay close attention to each play and not to anticipate or imagine action which had not occurred. He also reminded them to use their hand signals to communicate with one another as the crowd was apt to be especially large and loud. The cheers and yells of the fans, the bands playing would make for an exciting atmosphere. They were reminded not to get caught up in the hoopla, but to concentrate on their assignments.

After reviewing their assignments, they began to dress in the not-so-famous Zebra uniforms, the customary black and white striped shirts, white pants and black shoes and caps. Shortly after they dressed, they took to the field to inspect the playing surface and surrounding areas.

As this was the last Thursday in November, the grass in the middle of the field was no more. There was dirt on dirt from one 35-yard line to the opposite 35-yard line. All of the high school teams in Houston, both Black and white, had begun using the field in early September; therefore, the field was well-worn. Inspection also revealed that some of the turf in other areas was also worn. However, the condition of the field today seemed to show excessive wear. In addition to all of the high schools' use of the field for their football games, Texas Southern University, the University of Houston, and the professional team, the Houston Oilers, used the field for their home games. Most of the teams who played at Jeppesen knew of these conditions and made adjustments accordingly. They would wear shoes with longer or shorter spikes as needed in order to get better traction on the worn turf. The worn field did not seem to bother most players unless the field had received considerable rain before the game.

The Lion's team, led by quarterback Sylvester Armstrong and running backs Thurman Thomas, Thomas Crissmon, Eddie Hughes, and Nathaniel Ray had an easy time of it as Yates led 28-0 late in the third quarter. Yates went on to win the game 32-12 as the team pasted the Wildcats from the opening period till the end. An extremely large crowd, reported to be 37,000, was in attendance. The Wheatley fans who had anticipated a really close match saw it all go up in smoke as their signal caller, Dave Edgerly, had five of his passes intercepted. Fumbles by the Wildcat's running backs also contributed to their defeat as the Lions capitalized on several of their errors and scored. The Wildcats did not score until the fourth period, when Coach Walker pulled his starting quarterback and inserted his backup, who completed several passes to get the Wildcats in scoring position. Most Yates followers went away from this game overjoyed as they saw their Golden Lions complete their regular season with an 8-2 record. The Thanksgiving Day win allowed them to share the district title with the Wildcats. However, because of their victory over the Wildcats they would represent the district in bi-district play.

Officiating the game today was less stressful than some earlier Classics as Yates seemed to control the game with ease. The biggest challenge facing the officiating crew was getting to and from the dressing rooms before the game and at halftime. The huge crowd was loud and enthusiastic. There was plenty of pushing and shoving as the officials made their way to and from the field.

During play there was only one questionable call all afternoon. One of the Wheatley running backs lost control of the ball on a running play near the sideline. The head lineman indicated the ball went out of bounds, whereas the Yates players insisted they recovered the ball inbounds. Wheatley retained possession, but turned the ball over on downs after the next play. The rest of the afternoon was uneventful as Yates players controlled their opponents fairly easily.

Officiating any contest calls for the officials to use good judgment and position themselves by moving about the playing field. Officiating is a daunting task as most calls for infractions are made when the official is on the move. Many fans, however, tend to second-guess calls which go against their team. One must take into consideration that officials are well-trained for their jobs. For the most part, they are not in a stationary position as are the fans, so that what they see and what the fans see may be entirely different. Schoolboy games are played by teenagers who are gifted and well-conditioned, and most try very hard to play by the rules. Most respect the officials and try to abide by their guidance.

The "Turkey Day Classic" was unique in many ways, and the officials had one of the most important responsibilities of anyone involved in the affair. It was their responsibility to maintain order, direct players and coaches who were intense and excited and who wanted to win this contest for bragging rights until next year. The men with the Zebra-like uniforms did their best in most situations to officiate in such a way that their integrity, honesty and character remained intact.

The Selection Process

The individuals chosen to officiate the Classics were well-respected by the coaches and school officials. According to Lawrence Collins, former Supervisor of the Southwestern Athletic

Conference Officials Association and a previous member of the local association who officiated the Classic for six consecutive years said, "The men assigned to work the Classic had worked many games during the season. However, each head coach from Wheatley and Yates was allowed to pick two officials apiece to work the Classic." Most of the officials were affiliated with a college either as an attendee or a graduate, and some had played collegiate sports. All belonged to and were certified by an officials association known as the Southwest Officials Association. Lawrence "Bruz" Henry served as its supervisor for many years. Observers from the officials association were present during most games to assess the officiating skills of its members.

Below is a partial list of officials which was taken from local newspapers. The college or university from which the official graduated is also given. The newspaper listings of officials ceased after 1952.

1930	Bert (Paul Quinn) Referee; Scott (Wiley) Umpire; Nabrit (Morehouse) Head Linesman
1931	Law (Lincoln) Referee; Cavil (Wiley) Umpire; Sheppard (Wiley), Head Linesman
1941	Cavil (Wiley) Referee; Lights (Morehouse) Umpire; Ewell (Howard), Head Linesman; Grier (Hampton) Field Judge
1942	Whitted (West Virginia) Referee; Purnell (Southern) Umpire; Price (Wiley) Head Linesman; Stevenson (Tuskegee) Field Judge
1943	Purnell (Southern Referee); Johnson (Tuskegee) Umpire; Johnson (Tuskegee) Head Linesman; Parsons (Lincoln, Pa.); Stevenson (Tuskegee) Field Judge
1944-1951	Unavailable

1952   H.S. Chase, Referee; Allen Best, Umpire; Sam
            Cade, Head Linesman; Charles Moore, Field Judge;
            School not listed.
1953-1966 Unavailable

The officials were highly devoted to their jobs, well-respected by their communities, and educated professional men who worked very hard at their assigned tasks. Rarely were there confrontations on the field of play which they could not handle. The coaches thought highly of these men, and respect was accorded them on the field as well as off. Year-in and year-out these men performed their duties with pride and dignity, so much so that the players in the game followed their lead and instructions without question.

Chapter 9

LET THE GAMES BEGIN!

**Life should be enjoyable; too often we think
it's about achievement.
The truth is that making life enjoyable
is an achievement in itself.
—Unknown—**

The three high schools, Washington, Wheatley, and Yates, engaged in athletic competition with each other beginning in 1927, and they continue to compete against each other to this day. However, the Thanksgiving Day Classic ceased with the integration of public schools in 1967. Wheatley met Washington in the first Thanksgiving Day game; however, the three schools began a rotation of play on Thanksgiving which lasted until the mid-1940s. The rotation ceased, and the Wheatley vs. Yates Turkey Day Classic was born in 1946.

Fan interest was such that school rivalries had developed from the time Yates and Wheatley were established. Football fever is not new to Houston, and a fanbase of 1,000 in 1927 would be equivalent to one of 20,000 in 2011. The extent of press coverage given these football games was indicative of their popularity.

The reports which follow are excerpts from write-ups in the following newspapers: *The Houston Chronicle, The Forward Times, The Houston Informer, The Houston Post, and The Houston Press.* For specifics as to Line-ups players and their positions for each of the games, see Appendix I.

From the Beginning-You Are There!

Although the official Thanksgiving Day Classic did not begin until 1946, Yates and Wheatley played their first game in 1927, and their epic battles have continued until this day. A summary of each game, beginning with the first game provide background information leading up to the Classic. This period was a glorious time in the history of schoolboy football in Houston, a time which enriched the lives of countless fans in the entire Houston community. Although the games between Yates and Wheatley became known as the Turkey Day Classic in 1946, many games between Yates and Washington and Wheatley and Washington were captivating and exciting as well.

1927	Yates 20, Wheatley 6	Barr's Field

Nearly 1,000 fans, a mammoth crowd for this era, witnessed this first contest between the Wheatley Wildcats, coached by John Codwell, and the Yates Lions, coached by William Holland. Wheatley, the "new kid on the block" was in its first year of existence. The Lions were victorious on this first occasion. The game was played at old Barr's field located on Bonner Street just off Washington Avenue in the Heights.

Wheatley met Booker T. Washington's Golden Eagles on Thanksgiving Day, and were defeated by the Eagles 19-12.

1928	Yates 0, Wheatley 14	Barr's Field

Wheatley's revenge! In just two seasons Coach Codwell had molded a squad which utilized deception and intricate formations together with perfect coordination. Although Yates quarterback, and halfbacks showed exceptional skills, they gained little headway as Wheatley's defense bottled them up all afternoon. The Saturday, December 15 contest ended with the Wildcats holding the Lions scoreless for a 14-0 win. Coach Coldwell's Wildcats completely outplayed the Lions. In the beginning of the second quarter, the Wildcats took the ball at their own 40-yard line and marched to their first score. Wheatley scored again after blocking a Lion's kick; Yates recovered the ball in the end zone resulting in a safety for the Fifth Ward squad.

The Wildcat's final score came in the second half on an electrifying 85-yard kickoff return. The extra point try no good. Yates took the ball to Wheatley's one-yard line during the last four minutes of play only to be stopped four successive times.

1929	Yates 0, Wheatley 7	West End Park

For the second consecutive year Wheatley held the Yates Lions scoreless before an enthusiastic capacity crowd on Armistice Day.

The turnout of fans at West End Park was reported to be the largest to witness a Black schoolboy game in Texas and in the South. A rain soaked, muddy field made the footing poor the entire day.

Yates had two golden opportunities to score points, but missed one when they lost one ball on a fumble and the other where the ball went over on downs. The Wildcats scored in the second period on a pass play, then ran for the extra point. This was all of the scoring for the contest.

| 1930 | Yates 6, Wheatley 0 | Buffalo Stadium |

Yates rebounded to shut out Wheatley with a 6-0 victory in the rain at Buffalo Stadium. Over 1,000 rooters and spectators braved the chilling rain and temperatures to witness the Lions' victory. The muddy field was in such poor condition that it was most difficult to distinguish one team from the other. Early in the contest, the Third Ward boys out-played their opponents because of the stellar play of its defense. They put the Wildcats bunch on the defensive and kept them there.

| 1931 | Yates 0, Wheatley 14 | West End Park |

For the fourth consecutive year one team failed to score as Wheatley defeated Yates 14-0. The game was played at West End Park on Armistice Day. Both squads found it difficult to sustain drives early in the contest. Several fumbles by Yates killed any hopes of scoring early, and the Wildcats prevented the Lions from gaining any advantage. Wheatley put its passing attack into play, completely baffling the Lions as the Wildcats marched down the field. The Wildcats first score came by way of the forward pass engineered by the team's captain. Late in the fourth quarter the Wildcats drove home another touchdown.

The Thanksgiving Day contest, an annual tilt between Wheatley and Washington, was forfeited (Washington 1, Wheatley 0) because of a dispute over weather conditions and a muddy field. The coaches were John Codwell for Wheatley and R.G. Lockett for Washington.

| 1932 | Yates 13, Wheatley 6 | Buffalo Stadium |

Both teams found pay dirt in their sixth meeting; however, the mighty Lions prevailed in the contest 13-6. This game was played on a Thursday night at 8.00 p.m. in Buffalo Stadium, which was a baseball stadium constructed for the local minor league baseball team, the Houston Buffalos. Prior to the contest *the Houston Post* noted, "The novelty of the occasion, as well as the fact that more fans can be off from their work, is expected to add decidedly to the usual number who crowd the stands for the local exhibition of bitter but clean rivalry."(November 10, 1932). Other newspaper accounts reported both teams were evenly matched. The Lions scored first as a result of a Wheatley running back fumbling into the arms of a Yates player, who ran 30 yards for a touchdown. Hard running by Lion's backs and a series of penalties against Wheatley led to the Lions' second score. The Lions' defense held Wheatley all evening, and the sterling kicking of the punter kept the Wildcats deep in their own territory. Wheatley's lone score came on a pass play of 65 yards.

| 1933 | Yates 2, Wheatley 6 | Buffalo Stadium |

Wheatley bounced back on Armistice Day to defeat the Yates crew by a score of 6-2. According to *the Houston Informer,* the Yates-Wheatley contest was the greatest exhibition of deceptive football plays seen that season. It further described the game as the most thrilling, the most colorful, and probably the hardest fought ever staged by the two teams.

Wheatley put together a scoring drive from their 47-yard line in the first period. The extra point try failed, and the score was 6-0. Following the kick-off, the Third Ward squad put together a long drive of their own only to have it thwarted at the Wildcat's 16-yard line. There the Wildcats drew a 15-yard penalty, which placed the ball at their own one-yard line. With fourth down and 12 yards to go the Wildcats took a safety rather than chance punting and getting the punt blocked. That ended the scoring for the contest.

| 1934 | Yates 32, Wheatley 7 | Buffalo Stadium |

In the eighth meeting of the two teams, Yates defeated Wheatley in a lopsided contest 32-7. The Lion's victory brought the series to four victories each for the two schools. The Lions played keep-away all evening as they bottled up the Wheatley offensive unit, forcing numerous turnovers. Wheatley's players gave tremendous effort all evening, but they were no match for the swift, aggressive Lions.

| 1935 | Yates 20, Wheatley 14 | Buffalo Stadium |

Yates defeated the Wildcats for the second consecutive year by a score of 20-14. The Lions' victory gave them a 5-4 lead in the series. This game was tied twice in the contest with Yates taking an early lead on a 60-yard run. Wheatley immediately countered with a long pass which put the Wildcats in scoring position, and eventually scored on a series of running plays. Yates scored for their second time; however, Wheatley scored again to tie the game at 14 apiece. The most exciting play of the contest was made by a Lions' defensive back who intercepted a pass and ran 92 yards. The Lions scored another touchdown late in the fourth quarter to seal the victory.

| 1936 Yates 6, Wheatley 30, Yates 0, Wheatley 26 | Buffalo Stadium |

Wheatley defeated its arch rival the Yates Lions twice this year, once early in the season (30-6) and later in the season (26-0). In the earlier game the Wildcats rolled up 24 points in the first half. Shifty backs and hard running ripped holes in the Lions' front wall. The Wildcats did not allow a Lions' first down in the first half of play. The Lions only score came late in the contest on a 15 yard pass play.

The Wildcats went undefeated in the 1936 gridiron season, and they defeated the Terrell High Panthers of Fort Worth 18-0 for the coveted state title.

1937	Yates 7, Wheatley 8	Buffalo Stadium

The Wildcats won for the second year in a row. Wheatley defeated the Lions 8-7. *The Houston Post,* reported that approximately 8,000 holiday fans witnessed the thrilling contest. Wheatley scored first on a 15-yard pass play, but missed the extra point try. A bad snap from the Yates' center during the third quarter caused the Yates punter to be tackled for a safety. Yates scored late in the third quarter for its only score of the day. This victory for the Wildcats made its 16th win in a row over two seasons. It also made Wheatley city and state champions for the second year in a row.

1938	Yates 6, Wheatley 9	Buffalo Stadium

For the third consecutive year Wheatley defeated the Lions on Thanksgiving Day by a score of 9-6. Wheatley's first score came on a safety when a Lions' back was tackled in the end zone. Wheatley's second score came early in the second period on a running play. The extra point was booted, and Wheatley led 9-0. Yates then completed seven first downs and sustained a 60-yard drive for its only score of the afternoon. The second half of the game resembled the first with both teams fumbling opportunities to score. The game statistics revealed that Yates rushed and passed for more yards and had more first downs than did Wheatley; however fumbles prevented them from scoring additional points. Wheatley won the Negro city title.

| 1939 | Yates 2, Wheatley 6 | Buffalo Stadium |

Wheatley won in a donnybrook 6-2 over their arch rivals on a rain-soaked field. There were 8,200 fans who witnessed the contest Thanksgiving Day. This was the fourth consecutive city crown registered by the Wildcats. Both teams had battled on even terms in the first half. However, in the third period Yates attempted a punt from within its end zone. The punt was blocked, and Wheatley's fullback fell on the ball for a score. Yates fumbled again at its own 13-yard line, but held off Wheatley's drive. In the late stages of the game Yates' long march ended at the Wheatley two-yard line. Wheatley gave up a safety and the game ended.

| 1940 | Yates 12, Wheatley 9 | Buffalo Stadium |

Yates defeated Wheatley 12-9 at Buffalo Stadium on Thanksgiving Day as approximately 9,000 fans witnessed the contest. During the second period of play Yates scored first, but missed the extra point. Wheatley retaliated and with the extra point the Wildcats led 7-6. Yates' second tally came on a bullet like pass play ending their scoring for the evening. Wheatley drove deep into the Lions' territory only to be thwarted on downs. To preserve their lead, the Lions gave the Wildcats a safety. This enabled them to free kick from the 20-yard line, but ended the scoring for the evening.

| 1941 | Yates 0, Wheatley 7 | Buffalo Stadium |

On Thanksgiving Day more than 14,000 fans filled Buffalo Stadium to witness the Wildcats' 7-0 victory over the Lions for the Negro city and district titles. Coach Codwell's team had several opportunities to score, but managed only one touchdown. The Wildcat's quarterback surprised the Yates defense in the third period by faking a spin then darting through the line and streaking 43 yards to pay dirt. The extra point try was good. Earlier in the contest the Wildcats had tried a 17-yard field goal, but the ball sailed wide of the goal post. This game was the last Wheatley-Yates battle played in Buffalo Stadium. A new Public School Stadium being constructed would be ready for next years' battle.

1942	Yates 12, Wheatley 7	Public School Stadium

The Informer's headlines read "Yates Is Winner in Houston: 15,000 Fans See Lions Clip Cats for Two Titles". The final score was 12-7. Coach Andrew "Pat" Patterson's Lions won the city and district titles Thanksgiving Day before a sea of enthusiastic fans. The Lions outperformed the Wildcats in every department except punting. Wheatley's punter kicked several long spirals all day to the delight and cheers of the Wildcat fans. However, the Lions were too much for the "Cats" to handle. This was the first Thanksgiving Day game to be played in the newly constructed Houston Public School Stadium.

1943	Yates 21, Wheatley 0	Public School Stadium

For the second year in a row the Lions defeated their rivals from Fifth Ward. A crowd of 15,000 witnessed this Thanksgiving Day clash. The Lion's opened the scoring early in the contest as they capitalized on a Wildcat fumble at the 49-yard line. Several run and pass plays later the Lions found pay dirt.

Wheatley moved the ball down field on a series of plays, but their threat was squashed. A broken-field run of more than 40 yards ended at the one-yard line. The Lion's scored their second touchdown on the next play. Both teams traded possession in the second half; however, Yates was able to convert its final score late in the fourth period after a Wheatley pass was intercepted at the 40-yard line. Yates had piled up 11 first downs to Wheatley's five.

| 1944 | Yates 0, Wheatley 6 | Public School Stadium |

The Thanksgiving Day game was the second battle between the two foes this season. Yates had won the early contest. Wheatley brought one defeat to the contest, having lost its initial game of the season. According to *The Houston Informer,* the two schools played twice a year in 1935, 1936, 1942, and 1943. During the last two years the city and district championships had been determined by the winner. "The Wildcats take Lions 6-0; Meet San Antonio for Bi-district Plum" is *The Informer's* headline.

This win also marked the first time the Wildcats had defeated the Lions in the Public School Stadium since its opening in 1942. The Fifth Ward school capitalized upon a Lions' fumbles in the third period and converted the turnover into a score on the first play of the period. That was the only scoring of the afternoon, as both defenses played extremely well the entire contest. The largest fan turnout of 18,000 saw Wheatley's Coach Obie Williams win his first game against Yates as head Coach.

| 1945 | Yates 26, Wheatley 0 | Public School Stadium |

A crowd of more than 13,000 fans witnessed Yates' defeat of Booker T. Washington on Thanksgiving Day with a score of 12-0. The game against Wheatley came a week later. The Lions toppled the Wildcats 26-0 before 8,000 fans to win the city title. Yates' Coach Roger Lights saw his chargers outman the Wildcats all evening. George Drake of *The Informer* wrote, "The Lions were on the prowl, racking up their most decisive victory of the season and one of the easiest that they have ever won over a Wheatley team." Yates first score came early after an exchange of punts had given the Lions the ball on Wheatley's 45-yard line. A series of running plays resulted in the Lions' score. With time running out in the first half, the Lions' fumbled at the two-yard line, and Wheatley recovered to end another scoring threat.

A long 65-yard march in the third quarter saw the Lions score their next touchdown to make the final score 26-0. The Wildcat's only threat of the afternoon came when early in the first period they recovered a fumble on the Yates 40. The Wildcats made four first downs in a row, which carried the ball to the 15-yard line to have the drive end on an interception.

1946	Yates 12, Wheatley 6	Public School Stadium

Grid fans braved bad rainy weather to see the Lions defeat the Wildcats 9-0 in their early September encounter. The game was marred by costly penalties and fumbles on both sides because of the muddy field. Wheatley players were constantly slipping through Yates' offensive line to stop the Lions. But constant pressure applied by the Lions' players allowed them to control the game all evening. The first two periods of play found the Lion's knocking on the Wildcats' door only to have their efforts turned back by fumbles.

However, in the opening stanza of the third quarter the Wildcats received the kickoff, but were penalized for holding, which placed the ball at their two-yard line. Unable to move the ball, the Wildcats punted, but the Lions blocked the punt to score a safety. After a series of exchanges by both squads the third quarter ended with the score 2-0 in favor of the Lions. A Wheatley fumble on its own eight-yard line gave the Lions a golden opportunity to score. After losing 20 yards because of two successive penalties, the quarterback completed a pass for a touchdown. The extra point try was good, and the Lions went ahead 9-0. That series ended the scoring for the night.

The Thanksgiving tilt saw the Yates team come from behind late in the fourth quarter to defeat Wheatley 12-6. Wheatley had tied the score at 6-6 midway in the second stanza, forcing the Lions to drive late in the period to break the deadlock. Over the last 20 years Yates and Wheatley had battled on Thanksgiving Day several times. However, the rotation with Washington on Thanksgiving had ended in 1945, and the official Turkey Day Classic between Wheatley and Yates was initiated with today's game.

1947	Yates 12, Wheatley 6	Public School Stadium

Yates defeated Wheatley before a near capacity crowd on Thanksgiving 12-6. The win enabled the Lions to capture the City Negro High School grid championship.

1948	Yates 0, Wheatley 0	Public School Stadium

The third Turkey Day Classic clash resulted in a defensive battle between the two teams all afternoon; the result was a 0-0 tie. Both teams had had opportunities to score throughout the game, but turnovers, interceptions and interference calls prevented both squads from scoring. An estimated 17,500 fans witnessed the standoff.

1949	Yates 6, Wheatley 7	Public School Stadium

The Wheatley Wildcats, displaying grit, determination and a never-say-die spirit came from behind to win the Houston Negro High School football crown by edging Yates 7-6. A sell-out crowd of 21,000 fans witnessed the Turkey Day Classic in the Public School Stadium. Both schools scored during the second period. Yates drove to within inches of the goal line in the third period, but Wheatley held, and the ball went over on downs. Yates then scored, but the extra point try was blocked. Then Wheatley's quarterback completed a pass for 29 yards to set up the ensuing Wheatley touchdown. This touchdown and successful extra point concluded the scoring for the afternoon. Yates pushed to the Wheatley goal line from its own 21-yard line, but failed to score again.

| 1950 | Yates 23, Wheatley 6 | Public School Stadium |

Yates won the City and District Titles and kept its record perfect for the season. The Turkey Day game saw the Lions defeat the Wildcats 23-6. Coach Johnson of Yates and Coach Countee of Wheatley had their teams ready to play.

Yates played for the state title against Booker T. Washington of Dallas, whom they had defeated 19-12 in Houston earlier in the season. However, when the game was played in Dallas, Washington was victorious.

| 1951 | Yates 26, Wheatley 19 | Public School Stadium |

Yates triumphs before the largest crowd to witness a game in the Public School Stadium. Spectators numbering 28,000 saw Yates 6'7" quarterback lead the Lions to a 26-19 victory as he passed for three touchdowns and ran one in from the six yard line.

Wheatley made a game of it after trailing 20-0. In the fourth quarter Wheatley scored after intercepting a Yates pass at the three-yard line. The Wildcat's swift halfback streaked 45 yards on a pass play to score and another one of his teammates ran 21 yards to score their last touchdown. However, with only one minute to play and the score 26-19, Yates' interception of a Wheatley pass at the Yates' nine-yard line sealed the victory for the Lions.

| 1952 | Yates 0, Wheatley 12 | Public School Stadium |

"Wheatley is victorious 12-0" was the headline from *The Houston Informer,* as 23,000 fans witnessed the Wildcats throttle the Lions. The smooth passing quarterback threw a 13-yard strike late in the second quarter for a 6-0 score. One glue finger Wildcat receiver caught a 41-yard pass to set-up Wheatley's second touchdown late in the fourth quarter. A 23-yard scamper through the middle of the Lions' defense capped a 73-yard march for the final score of the afternoon. The Wildcat's victory enabled them to be crowned City Negro football champions as they defeated Yates for the first time since 1949. Yates 6'7" quarterback, scrambled all afternoon for a total of 82 yards to lead all ground carriers. The only Yates penetration came during the third period, as they marched the ball 67-yards only to fumble it away at the two-yard line and Wheatley recovered.

| 1953 | Yates 22, Wheatley 16 | Public School Stadium |

The third largest paid attendance, 23,252 fans ever to witness the Turkey Day Classic was treated to the pass oriented Yates offense as the Lions defeated the Wildcats 22-16. Yates passing attack accounted for 196 yards and three touchdowns. A number of glue fingered receivers caught most of the passes thrown to them all day. Both teams gave up safeties early in the contest.

Wheatley came storming back in the third period with a 17-yard score to tie the contest. However, the Lion's passing duo again did their number, which covered 32 yards and a score. The point after was good. The score was 16-9 in favor of the Lions at this point. Wheatley was not finished for the afternoon as they scored again on a 32-yard pass play to close the gap. But the Lions rebounded and scored again on a magnificent one-handed catch to end the scoring for the afternoon.

| 1954 | Yates 15, Wheatley 14 | Public School Stadium |

"Yates upsets Wheatley 15-14" was the headlines of *The Houston Post*. This game turned-out to be one of the most thrilling games between the two rivals in all of their matchups. Early in the first period Wheatley scored first as Yates fumbled on the Wildcats 39-yard line. The ball flipped into the air and was caught by a defensive player who rambled 61 yards for a touchdown. The extra point try was good.

The Lions got on the scoreboard in the second period with a pass caught in the end zone, but the point after was blocked, and Wheatley retained a 7-6 lead. Midway through the second period, Yates advanced the ball deep in Wildcat territory. The Wildcats defense stopped the Lions at the seven-yard line on each of three tries. The Lions kicked a field goal and took a 9-7 lead.

The Wildcats came back in the third period when the Lions attempted a punt from their own four-yard line. The punt was blocked, and the Wildcats recovered the football. After three tries and no luck the Wildcat fullback rammed it over the goal line, and Wheatley led 14-9. Late in the fourth quarter Lion's quarterback passed for 28 yards and a series of runs advanced the ball to the four-yard line, where the fullback scored giving the Lions a 15-14 advantage. The win enabled the Lions to be crowned City champs. It was a bitter loss for Wheatley, its first of the season. However, the Wildcats went on to represent the district and win the state championship over Moore High School of Waco.

| 1955 | Yates 0, Wheatley 0 | Public School Stadium |

A record number of 24,437 fans witnessed the scoreless tie between Yates and Wheatley. The two schools were crowned co-champions for the City title. Although the game was a scoreless tie, the Lions had opportunities to score as they were inside Wheatley's 20-yard line on three occasions, but could not move the pigskin to "pay dirt". The Lions' quarterback completed 13 of 26 passes, whereas the Wildcat's quarterback completed only 6 of 14. Late in the fourth quarter one of Wheatley's finest linemen intercepted a Lion s' pass at the 9-yard line to thwart the Lions' last effort to score. The final season record for each team, for Yates 5-3-2 and for Wheatley 8-1-1.

1956	Yates 18, Wheatley 21	Public School Stadium

Precision passing led the Wheatley Wildcats to a 21-18 victory over the Yates Lions before 22,221 fans on Thanksgiving. Wheatley trailed 18-7 at halftime; however the Fifth Ward crew was able to power their way to win the contest and the covered City title.

The Lions scored early when a running back returned a punt 68-yards for the Lions' first touchdown. Yates kicker failed on all three of his point after tries for the afternoon. A pass for 34 yards secured the Lions' second touchdown. The quarterback scored the Lions' third touchdown on a three-yard run late in the first half.

Climaxing an 85-yard drive, the Wildcat's rammed over from the one-yard line for Wheatley's first score before halftime. Another 63-yard drive by the Wildcats netted their second scoring drive and a seven-yard touchdown. The Wildcats last tally came in the fourth quarter on another 63-yard drive. They scored the extra point on an end run after a bad snap from center. Yates had its final drive killed late in the fourth quarter by the interception of a pass on the Wildcat's 13-yard line, which ended the scoring for the afternoon.

| 1957 | Yates 12, Wheatley 6 | Public School Stadium |

Yates' season ending record stood at 8-2, whereas Wheatley's record was 8-1-1. Before 26, 832 fans the Lions opened the scoring in the second period by moving the ball from their own 44-yard line by means of a pass of 39-yards and a subsequent run of 24-yards for the score, but the extra point try was missed. Early in the second quarter the Wildcats had two drives thwarted by the agile Yates forward wall. One drive ended at the Yates' 16-yard line, and the other ended at the Yates' eight-yard line because of an intercepted pass.

Opening the third period of play the Wildcats kicked off to the Lions who returned the ball to their own 12-yard line. On the first play from scrimmage Yates fumbled the ball, which the Wildcats recovered. Four plays later the Wildcats managed to run for a touchdown, but the extra point try was missed. Yates' second score came quickly after the Wildcat's touchdown. Yates quarterback heaved a 61-yard bomb for a touchdown, which ended the scoring for the afternoon. The Lions' victory helped the 9-0-1 Booker T. Washington Eagles win the district title to face L. C. Anderson of Austin in the semifinal state playoff run.

| 1958 | Yates 8, Wheatley 20 | Pubic School Stadium |

A day before the contest key players from both teams were ruled ineligible for play. An estimated crowd of 22,000 rain-soaked fans witnesses the Wildcats defeat the Lions 20-8. During the first quarter of play, the Lions scored on a pass play and another pass for the two point conversion. With 2:25 remaining in the initial quarter, a Wildcat halfback ripped the Lions' defense and galloped 56 yards to pay dirt. The Wildcats' attempt to run the extra point conversion failed. Yates led at halftime 8-6. Wheatley scored 14 points in the second half and held the Lions scoreless.

The Wildcats' final two scores came on runs of 10-yards and five-yards. A two point conversion was successful.

1959	Yates 0, Wheatley 28	Public School Stadium

The Wildcat 28-0 lopsided victory over the Lions before 22,283 fans was hard for the Lions' faithful to swallow. The Wildcats scored in the first three quarters and threatened in the fourth period. Defensive stalwarts led the Wildcats and shut out the Lions all day. A fumble by Yates resulted in a recovery by the Wildcats which resulted in their first score of the day. A run for the two-point conversion failed. The Cats also scored on a safety when their tenacious defensive players tackled a Lion in the end zone.

In the second period a halfback scored from the two and converted the extra point to put the Wildcats ahead 15-0. The Wildcats scored two more touchdowns, and converted an extra point to end the days scoring.

1960	Yates 0, Wheatley 3	Public School Stadium

The Wheatley faithful were overjoyed as their Wildcats subdued the Lions 3-0 for the second consecutive Thanksgiving day victory, as a crowd of 29,000 fans witnessed the contest. The Wildcats kicked a 10-yard field goal midway the third period, which was all that was needed to win this one. With only nine second left in the contest Yates field-goal try for a tie failed as the ball sailed three yards wide of its mark. Yates had five separate drives deep in Wheatley's territory all afternoon, but could not push the ball into the end zone for a score. Statistically the Lions outperformed the Wildcats in every category except punting and scoring. The Cat's punter kicked the ball deep into Lion's territory all afternoon to keep them pended down.

| 1961 | Yates 21, Wheatley 15 | Public School Stadium |

More than 40,000 fans saw Yates defeat Wheatley by a score of 21-15. Newspaper accounts reported attendance to have been the largest to witness a schoolboy football game in Texas and anywhere else except an all-star game in Chicago. The Wildcats had a case of fumblitis as they turned the ball over four times. The Lions capitalized on three of them for scores. Three different players were credited with scoring the Lion's touchdowns.

The Wildcats drove the ball 25yards for their first tally, and 59 yards for their second touchdown. The extra point try was good. Both teams entered the contest with perfect records. Yates won the bi-district game against Hebert of Beaumont, but lost the state contest 19-13 to Anderson High of Austin.

| 1962 | Yates 32, Wheatley 12 | Public School Stadium |

The Yates quarterback, lead the Lions to a 32-12 drubbing of the Wildcats before 37,000 holiday fans. The Lions' first score was set-up by a pass interception, followed by a series of passes and runs. The point-after try was good. Wheatley fumble the ball at the 16-yard line and five play later the Lions scored from the four-yard line. The quarterback passed for a two point conversion, and the Lions led 15-0.

Before halftime the Lions' intercepted another Wildcats pass and advanced to the Wildcats' 24-yard line. Yates quarterback completed another one of his passes for 20-yards to score and the Lions led 21-0. Late in the third quarter the Lions advanced the ball from the Wildcats' 47-yard line, and covered the distance in six plays to increase its lead to 28-0. The Lions scored again after another Wheatley fumble, and the accurate passing of Yates' quarterback completed another pass for eight yards and a touchdown. Wheatley' substitute quarterback moved the ball well for a 22-yard completion to the Lions' two-yard line. The Wildcats scored on the next play. With less than two minutes to play, the Wildcats scored again on a one-yard plunge. The two point conversion try failed. Yates' victory enabled them to represent the district in the bi-district playoff. Moreover, the Lions were victorious in the playoff as they captured the state championship.

1963	Yates 21, Wheatley 14	Public School Stadium

Both squads were ready for battle as they returned from their hideaways. Yates' team was secluded at Prairie View, and Wheatley's team was at Camp Holden. The coaches took to secluding their teams because of the many distractions in town the night before the big game. The rain on Wednesday and Thanksgiving day did not hamper the golden Lions' determination as they defeated the Wildcats 21-14. Some 19,864 fans braved the inclement weather to watch the Lions bowl over the Wildcats for the third consecutive year.

All of Yates' scores came in the second period. The first score followed a high snap from center over the head of the punter, who was tackled at the Wildcats' 27-yard line. The Yates quarterback, zipped a perfect spiral to a lone receiver for the touchdown. An interception set up the second score as the Lions returned the ball to the Wildcats' 15-yard line. The Lions scored on two successive runs from that point, and once again before halftime.

Wheatley also scored before halftime on a 68-yard drive engineered by its quarterback, who threw a scoring pass from nine yards out. The two-point conversion was successful. Wheatley's last score came on a 14-yard pass play, which capped a 90-yard drive in the last period. Another two point try failed. Wheatley's last drive ended at the Yates 30-yard line as time expired.

The Lions' victory enabled them to meet Galveston Central Bearcats in bi-district play the next week. Galveston Central defeated the Lions 24-20.

1964   Yates 25, Wheatley 0   Public School Stadium

Before 22,478 holiday fans, the Yates Lions throttled the Wheatley Wildcats 25-0. Yates began the assault when one of its nifty receivers caught a 36-yard pass and four plays later Yates scored on another pass play. After intercepting a Wheatley pass, the Lions 'players again thrilled its faithful with a 78-yard scoring play, however the point-after was no good, and the Lions led 13-0. Another Lions' drive ended with a fumble on the Wildcats' 16-yard line. On the first play of the fourth quarter the Lions' completed a 53-yards slant play for a touchdown. The last of the scoring came on a 14-yard pass play.

Wheatley's lone scoring attempt came after the initial kickoff and ended at Yates' 20-yard line.

1965   Yates 7, Wheatley 6   Public School Stadium

For the fifth consecutive year the Lions defeated the Wildcats 7-6. Yates' only score came midway the first quarter when a bad snap sailed over the head of the Wildcats' quarterback who was tackled on the 15-yard line. Two plays later, the Lions' converted a short pass to the end zone for a touchdown. The extra-point kick was good for a 7-0 lead.

Yates had several other opportunities to score, but the Wildcats' defense refused to let them into the end zone. The Lions had drives end at the Wildcat's 5, 22, and 24-yard lines. The Wildcats also saw two of their drives end at the Lions' 38 and 9-yard line. The Wildcats scored in the third period on a Yates bobbled football recovered by the Wildcats on the Lions' 25-yard line. A reserve quarterback for the Wildcats threw a 25-yarder for a touchdown. The all-important extra-point try sailed wide, and that miss ended the scoring for the afternoon. Some 26,000 fans witnessed the contest.

1966	Yates 6, Wheatley 3	Public School Stadium

This year's matchup would be the last game to be played on Thanksgiving day. Some 28,121 paying fans turned out to witness the historic last Turkey Day Classic. For the sixth consecutive year the Lions defeated the Wildcats 6-3. The record books reveal that Yates had won 24 of 46 games played during the past 40 years, and three games ended in ties. Also there were several years when the two schools met twice during the season.

Wheatley scored first in the third period after a brilliant fumble recovery on the Lion's 13-yard line. Following two running plays, Wheatley's quarterback kicked a field goal from a very difficult angle to put the Wildcats ahead 3-0. Wheatley had several opportunities to score at various points in the game on Yates' fumbles, but the Lion's defense would have none of that. With 5:39 left in the contest the Lions offense came alive. A screen pass covered 56-yards to the Wildcats' 25-yard line. Five plays later Yates' fullback, rammed into the end zone for a touchdown. The extra point try was wide, but the Lions were ahead 6-3, ending the scoring for the day.

The Turkey Day Classic with all its splendor and glory ended on Thanksgiving day 1966. Throughout the years beginning in 1927 many football fans were treated to epic battles between the Fifth Ward and Third Ward high schools. It was always a give and take battle between the schools. The actions of each squad were fierce with strong defensive maneuvers and innovated offensive tactics highlighting play. The outcome of this game determined on many occasions the City and/or district champions. As the games began rivalries were created, a Classic born, now ended after 39 glorious years.

1962-63 Classic. It's A Fumble

Queens of Yesteryear

1962-63 Classic. Get ready for action

The crowning of Miss Wheatley during halftime

Miss Wheatley and her court during halftime

Wheatley's Band Majorettes 'prancing and dancing' along sideline
during halftime

Wheatley attempts extra point during 1957-58 Classic

Wheatley's Fullback (#31) James Taylor skirts left end 1957-58

Yates and Wheatley team captains before the game 1957-58

November 26, 1966   FORWARD TIMES, Houston, Texas

LEO TAYLOR (YATES)   GEORGE FOUNTAIN(YATES)   RONALD REED(YATES)

**All Photos
By Provost
Studio**

Yates players in 1966-67 Classic

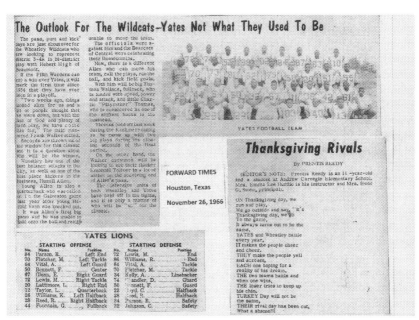

The Outlook For The Wildcats—Yates Not What They Used To Be

The pass, punt and kick' days are just about over for the Wheatley Wildcats who are looking to represent district 3-4A in bi-district play with Hebert High of Beaumont.

If the Fifth Warders can cop a win over Yates, it will mark the first time since 1954 that they have ever been in a playoff.

"Two weeks ago, things looked slim for us and a lot of people thought that we were down, but with the help of God and plenty of hard play, we have come this far," The mild-mannered Frank Walker stated.

Records are thrown out of the window for this classic and it is a question about who will be the winner. Wheatley has one of the best holster attacks in the city, as well as one of the best place kickers in the business, Thaxell Allen.

Young Allen is also a quarterback who was called on in the Galveston game last year after young Harold Vann was knocked out.

It was Allen's first big game and he was unable to hold onto the ball and really

unable to move the team.

The officials were against him and the Bearcats of Central were celebrating their Homecoming.

Now, there is a different Allen who can move his team, call the plays, run the ball, and kick field goals.

With him will be big Thomas Wallace, fullback, who is loaded with speed, power and attack, and little Charlie "Playmaker" Thomas, who is considered as one of the shiftiest backs in the business.

Thomas paid off last week during the Kashmere outing as he came up with two big plays during the closing seconds of the final period.

On the other hand, the Walker crewmen will be looking to use their flanker Emanuel Toliver in a lot of action on the receiving end of Allen's pass.

The defensive units of both Wheatley and Yates have paid off in the tights, and it is only a matter of who will be "up" for the classic.

YATES FOOTBALL TEAM

Thanksgiving Rivals

By PRENTIS REEDY

(EDITOR'S NOTE: Prentis Reedy is an 11-year-old and a student at Andrew Carnegie Elementary School. Mrs. Emma Lee Hurdle is his instructor and Mrs. Irene G. Stone, principal.)

ON Thanksgiving day, we run and play,
We go outside and say, "It's Thanksgiving day, we go
To the game,
It always turns out to be the same,
YATES and Wheatley battle every year,
IT makes the people cheer and cheer,
THEY make the people yell and scream,
EACH one hoping for a reality of his dream,
THE two teams battle and when one wins,
THE loser tries to keep up his chin,
TURKEY Day will not be the same,
THEIR rival day has been cut, What a shame!!!

FORWARD TIMES

Houston, Texas

November 26, 1966

YATES LIONS

	STARTING OFFENSE			STARTING DEFENSE	
No.	Name	Position	No.	Name	Position
84	Parson, R.	Left End	72	Lewis, M.	End
70	Fletcher, M.	Left Tackle	86	Williams, R.	End
64	Vital, A.	Left Guard	64	Vital, A.	Tackle
50	Bennett, F.	Center	70	Fletcher, M.	Tackle
67	Glenn, E.	Right Guard	34	Kelly, A.	Linebacker
72	Lewis, M.	Right Tackle	74	Candler, D.	Guard
20	Lattimore, L.	Right End	50	Bennett, F.	Guard
12	Taylor, L.	Quarterback	22	Boyd, C.	Halfback
26	Williams, K.	Left Halfback	28	Reed, R.	Halfback
28	Reed, R.	Right Halfback	84	Parson, R.	Safety
44	Fountain, G.	Fullback	32	Johnson, C.	Safety

Yates team photo 1966-67 and poem by Prentis Reedy

Hail Wheatley, Yates Queens Of Yesteryear

Queens of Yesteryear

HAIL THE QUEENS – It was a grand old day for the former high school queens of both Wheatley and Yates, Thanksgiving Day as both schools paid tribute to the many queens of yesteryear.

During the halftime show at the last annual Turkey Day Classic, between Wheatley and Yates, all of the queens that could be present during the game were honored along with the first captain of both the Lions and Wildcat football teams.

Wheatley will long remember names like Wilma Hogan, the first queen; Mary Tann, Jewell Phillips, Beatrice Crostley, Edna Craig,

Williams, Leola Struss, Margaret Hall, Bessie Anderson, Minnie Ryan, Evelyn Beal, Joan Bookman, Arnetta Faine, Angelia Moore, Natalie Osborne, Charlene Kelly, Jean Walton, Charlie Mae Hainey, Daisy Jacques, and Bell Millard.

For the golden Lions were Vivian Day, Jewell Brown, Maxine Bullock, Gloria Vernay, Lenola Neveu, Gertrude Stone, Patricia Jolivet, Carolyn Wilkins, and Helena Chester. These are just a few of the names that will be long remembered. (All staff photos by Artice "Cboy" Vaughn)

Queens of Yesteryear

Yates band plays for Yates-Wheatley Classic

Yates Band begins halftime activities 1953-54

Wheatley's Marching Band 1956-57

Wheatley's Purple and White Squadron 1956-57

The Royal Family

Pageboy Martin Guillory, *Miss Wheatley*, Mary Tapp, her *escort* John Hartwell, *Attendants*, Geraldine DeLoach; Doro-

Mary Trapp Miss Wheatley 1956-57

Miss Yates and her Attendants

Parade float with Wanda Proctor Miss Yates and Court 1957-58

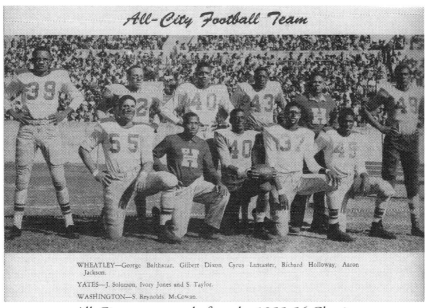

Helicopter on the field with Carolyn Wilkins Miss Yates and Court
1958-59

All-City Football Team

WHEATLEY—George Balthazar, Gilbert Dixon, Cyrus Lancaster, Richard Holloway, Aaron
Jackson.
YATES—J. Solomon, Ivory Jones and S. Taylor.
WASHINGTON—S. Reynolds. McCowan.

All-City team pose before the 1955-56 Classic

Left to right: Sanders Williams, Miss Norma Bazeron, Miss Wande Procter, John Walker, Miss Vera Bradley, George Allen, Miss Josie Haller, Miss Ezola Broussard, Charles Batiste, Miss Thelma Robins, Mrs. James D. Ryan, Dean Ethel C. Ellison and Principal William S. Holland.

Josie Haller Miss Yates and Court 1953-54

ROBERT McGOWEN scores first touchdown against Wheatley.

1953 McGowen scores Yates first touchdown

Head Coach Frank Walker, Wister Lee, Felix Cook and R. Countee.

Wheatley Coaching Staff 1956-57

Yates Coaching Staff 1962-63

Classic action 1964-65

Chapter 10

EPILOGUE

**I have learned that life may not always be easy
But it's always worth living.
—Melanie Race—**

The individuals who had the opportunity to compete as athletes or perform as band members, drill squad members, and cheerleaders as well as the spectators who witnessed these games mourn their passing. The Classic has become a fleeting memory in the minds of those who lived during that era. Segregation and Jim Crow laws were indirectly responsible for the game's reaching the magnitude and height of its success. Because of segregation Blacks were largely confined to their communities and the activities which took place therein. The larger Houston community's cultural, sports and social events were in many respects off-limits to Blacks. Therefore, an event like the Thanksgiving Day Classic was developed by Blacks for Blacks.

These games and accompying activities served as some of the most important cultural events in the Black community, allowed members of the Black community to exert control over these activities as everyday life was stymied by segregation. These games allowed Blacks to come together and celebrate their culture, develop racial pride, and promote community unity outside the controls of white society. Homer McCoy, a teacher and businessman in the community, called the game "High School's greatest spectacle."

The majority of the Black community in Houston was congregated within the three Wards. The three high schools for Blacks were located in these Wards. As the communities grew, the population of the schools grew, and natural rivalries developed. Fierce loyalties and competition developed among the three schools, Booker T. Washington, Phillis Wheatley and Jack Yates, and escalated each year beginning with their first athletic meetings in 1927.

In the early years Wheatley played Washington on Thanksgiving Day, and Yates Played Wheatley on Armistice Day, and Yates played Washington on Christmas. Beginning in the mid-1930s, the three schools began to rotate as to which teams would play on Thanksgiving. Sometime in the mid-1940s, because of the revenue generated by the huge crowds in annual attendance at Yates vs. Wheatley football games and because of lobbying by Yates' and Wheatley's principals, the Yates vs. Wheatley game on Thanksgiving, evolved into the Thanksgiving Day Classic. In most circles the game was referred to as "The Turkey Day Classic".

Were there other schoolboy games during this era which equaled in attendance the Thanksgiving Day Classic? It was reported in one of the local newspapers that only one other schoolboy game, one held in Chicago, came close to rivaling this Classic. Moreover, the Chicago game was not a regularly scheduled game between opponents each year, but rather an all-star game between public schools and private schools.

The Thanksgiving Day Classic reached its zenith during the late 1950s and early 1960s as attendance figures rose into 20,000 plus each year. In 1957 a total of 30,000 plus fans attended, and in 1961 over 40,000 fans were reported. Reporting of game attendance figures in some instances was not accurate. One explanation was that HISD officials asked that the true count not be reported because the number of fans exceeded the capacity of the stadium in violation of fire code restrictions.

With the integration of public schools in Houston, all school extracurricular activities came under the University Interscholastic League (UIL) beginning in 1967. The UIL policies were such that all district games had to be completed before Thanksgiving Day as the state playoffs would then be in progress. This policy brought an end to the Thanksgiving Day Classic. The Black citizens of Houston, particularly those in the Third and Fifth Wards, had mixed emotions about the demise of their Classic. This turn of events was seen as progress for the Blacks who had pushed for integration; yet they longed to continue this rivalry on Thanksgiving Day which had existed for nearly 40 years. Did the fans, alumni and supporters of both schools mourn the passing of the Classic? Surely they did, as there would not be another cultural event in the community which would be so uniquely theirs-in conception and implementation—one which provided such pageantry, and splendor, that the Thanksgiving Day Classic provided. Henceforth, *Requiem for a Classic.* Memories and reminiscences would exist only as a Requiem.

Appendix I

The Line-Ups

The Line-ups are provided through 1966, however several years the information was not available including: 1927, 1928, 1932, 1934, 1936, 1937, 1938, 1944, 1946, 1947, 1948, 1950, 1959, 1960, 1961, 1962, and 1965. Notes concerning outstanding players are also provided. This information was found in *The Houston Chronicle, The Forward Times, The Houston Informer,* and *The Houston Post.*

1927—Outstanding players
   Yates—Williams, Davis, M. Davis, Howard
   Wheatley—Fairfax and Hubbard

The Houston Informer (November 5, 1927)

1928—Outstanding players
   Yates—Burr, Riley, Russell and Williams
   Wheatley—Fairfax, R. Hubbard, Lastera and Sims

The Houston Informer (November, 1928)

1929 LINE-UPS

Wheatley	Position	Yates
Sims	Left End	Johnson
Peeble	Left Tackle	Davis
Green	Left Guard	Davis
Holland	Center	Jones
Laster	Right Guard	Winn
Mack	Right Tackle	Pinson
Collier	Right End	Franklin
Hubbard	Quarterback	Williams
Carroll,	Left Halfback	Ward
Armstrong,	Right Halfback	Eldridge
Jefferson	Fullback	Grant

The Houston Informer (November, 1929)

Outstanding players

Yates—Grant, Sanders, Eldridge,
Wheatley—Hubbard, Sims, Jefferson

1930 LINE-UPS

Wheatley	Position	Yates
Sims	LE	Perry
Qualls	LT	Davis
Green	LG	Winn
McGruder	C	Jones
Lastera	RG	Pettis
Thomas	RT	Watkins
Armstrong	RE	Gatson
Hubbard	QB	Williams
Carroll	LH	Murray
Haywood	RH	Ward
Mack	FB	Bryant

The Houston Informer (November 15, 1930)

1931 LINE-UPS

Wheatley	Position	Yates
Smith	LE	Demaris
Lewis	LT	Robinson
Butler	LG	Taylor
Edwards	C	Greenleaf
Lastera (captain)	RG	Winn
Holmes	RT	Lewis
Armstrong	RE	Gaston
Henry	QB	Williams (captain)
Williams	LH	Bryant
Lewis	RH	Eldredge
Hubbard	FB	Jones

The Houston Informer (November 14, 1931)

1932—Outstanding players
Yates—Millard, Williams, Brown,
Wheatley—W. Williams, J. Williams

The Houston Informer (November, 1932)

1933 LINE-UPS

Wheatley	Position	Yates
Jackson	LE	Davis
Lewis	LT	Perry
Fair	LG	Taylor
Payne	C	Grovey
Hulitt	RG	McConico
Thomas	RT	Lewis
Edwards	RE	Smith

Williams	QB	Ward
Harvey	LH	Neyland
Lewis	RH	Howard
Sneed	FB	Henderson

The Houston Informer (November 1933)

1934—Outstanding players

Yates—Grovey, Hollins, Burton, McGriff, Pickett, Hill.
Wheatley—Payne, Wyatt, Montgomery, Landry, Joseph, Smith.

1935 LINE-UPS

Wheatley	Position	Yates
Joseph	LE	Spiller
McGar	LT	Asbury
Henderson	LG	Byrd
Payne	C	Holland
Montgomery	RG	Bouldin
Eaton	RT	Sheldon
Gibson	RE	Jackson
Walker	Q	Makey
Smith	LH	Hill
Murray	RH	Huckey
Gary	FB	Norman

Outstanding players

Yates—Kindle, Hill, Makey, Hickey, McGriff
Wheatley—Smith, Sanders, Walker, Joseph, Edwards, Gibson, Hodges

The Houston Post (November 22, 1935)

1936 Outstanding players
>**Yates**—Kindle, Hope
>**Wheatley**—Smith, Allen, Murry, Wyatt, Hodge, Marcell

1938 Outstanding players
>**Yates**—Davis, Ross, Harris, Williams
>**Wheatley**—Lane, Young, Lindsay.

The Informer (December 3, 1938)

1939 LINE-UPS

Yates	Position	Wheatley
Gross	Left End	Kelly
Dade	Left Tackle	Murray
Cross	Left Guard	Holmes
Wilson	Center	Nash
Payne	Right Guard	Pear
Clifton	Right Tackle	Smith
De Batto	Right End	Alonzo
Williams	Quarterback	Grimes
Hamilton	Left Halfback	Deramus
Davis	Right Halfback	Lindsay
Ross	Fullback	Green

The Houston Chronicle (December 1, 1939)

1940 LINE-UPS

Wheatley	Position	Yates
Lofton	Left End	Jones
McCullough	Left Tackle	Morgan
Moore	Left Guard	Adams
Nash	Center	Boney
Coffee	Right	Guard Boone

Castilla	Right Tackle	Strayham
Tucker	Right End	Anderson
Dorsey	Quarterback	J. Jones
Scott	Left Half	Moses
Johnson	Right Half	Harris
Aldridge	Fullback	Ross

The Houston Chronicle (November 28, 1940)

Outstanding players
Yates—Jones, Harris, Burnett
Wheatley—Aldridge, Scott, Johnson, Dorsey, McCullough

1941 LINE-UPS

Wheatley	Position	Yates
Dodd	LE	Anderson
McCullough	RT	Moses
Castillo	LG	Adams
Nash	C	Strayhan
McCullough	RT	Morgan
Hampton	RG	Gilliyard
Loftin	RE	Carr
Fox	QB	Davis
Gibson	RH	Jones
Scott	LH	Burnett
Aldridge	FB	Harris

The Houston Post (November 28, 1941)

1942 LINE-UPS

Wheatley	Position	Yates
Sims	Left End	Wilson
Young	Left Guard	Haller
Dixon	Left Tackle	Moses
Gash	Center	Thomas
Coffey	Right Guard	H. Thomas
Cook	Right Tackle	Gilyard
Lofton	Right End	Green
Fox	Quarterback	Davis
McCauley	Left Half	Burnett
Gipson	Right Half	Jones
Sample	Full Back	James

The Houston Informer (December 5, 1942)

1943 LINE-UPS

Wheatley	Position	Yates
Robert Scott	Left End	Jeff Jennings
M.C. Simms	Left Tackle	Frank Hunter
Curtis Leroy	Left Guard	Lawrence Haller
James Gash	Center	Jimmy Gamble
Thomas White	Right Guard	J. B. Keyes
Felix Cook	Right Tackle	Willie Moses
C. Simms	Right End	Alex Martin
G. Jones	Quarterback	John Davis
E. Davis	Left Half	R. Ross
S. Barnum	Full Back	J. Lawson

The Houston Informer (December 4, 1943)

Outstanding players
> **Yates**—Peoples, Moses, Davis, Ross.
> **Wheatley**—Scott, Davis, Cook, Barnum.

1945 LINE-UPS

Wheatley	Position	Yates
Scott	Left End	HarryWoodard
L. Marshall	Left Tackle	Frank Thomas
H. Garner	Left Guard	Frazier Richmond
W. Miller	Center	Jimmy Gamble
T. White	Right Guard	Bennie White
A. Adams	Right Tackle	Ewell Crozier
R. Tapscott	Right End	James Rucker
B. McCauley	Quarterback	Raymond Daniels
L. Sheppard	Left Half	Robert Ross
E. Davis	Right Half	W. Woodard
R. Robinson	Fullback	Arthur Jackson

The Houston Informer (December 8, 1945)

Outstanding players
> **Yates**—Daniels, Jackson, Woodard, White, Richmond, Gamble, Thomas
> **Wheatley**—Davis, Sheppard, McCauley, Robinson, Scott, Adams, Miller.

1946—Outstanding players
> **Yates**—Daniels, Johnson, Roy, Dotson, Johnson.
> **Wheatley**—Simpson, Tapscott, Marshall, Adams

The Informer (November, 1946)

1949 LINE-UPS

Wheatley	Position	Yates
Johnny Glover	Left End	J. Henry
Scott	Left Tackle	Timms
Collins	Left Guard	Robinson
Bedford	Center	Spivey
Bower	Right Guard	Hatcher
Porter	Right Tackle	Randon
Belcher	Right End	BennieRoy
Joseph Linton	Quarterback	Alva Hayes
James Morris	Left Half	Otis Henry
Luther Robinson	Right Half	Joe Martel
Marshall Washington	Full Back	Ernest Dumas Lang

The Houston Informer (November 26, 1949)

Outstanding players

Yates—Collins, Martel, Lang.
Wheatley—Porter, Linton, Gloves, Rems.

1951 LINE-UPS

Wheatley	Position	Yates
Seab Blaylock	End	Nate Johnson
Melvin White	End	James Brooks
Johnny Boone	Tackle	Joe Dixon
Harold Trahan	Tackle	Horace Davis
Lionel Blount	Guard	Henry Hackett
Leroy Jackson	Guard	Artis Franklin
Johnny Marks	Center	Lee Brooks
George Campbell	Quarterback	George Gray
Adrian Gould	Halfback	O.C. Merchinson
James Green	Halfback	Edward Murray
Arthur Chambers	Fullback	Robert Scroggins

The Houston Informer (Nov. 24, 1951)

Outstanding players
Yates—Gray, Murray, Johnson.
Wheatley—White, Fielder

1952 LINE-UPS

Wheatley	Position	Yates
Gorden Gibson	LE	David Mitchell
Frank Breader	LT	Robert Terry
Leroy Jackson	LG	Willie Scott
Willie Williams	C	William McQueen
Robert Conley	RG	Clarence Hines
Wilbur Hegger	RT	Arthur Smith
David Brown	RE	Johnny Price
George Campbell	Q	George Gray
Johnny Felder	LH	Edward Murray
James Green	RH	Earl Young
Robert Elijah	FB	Nathan Bonham

The Houston Informer (November, 1952)

1953 LINE-UPS

Wheatley	Position	Yates
Bell, Ford, Gipson, Edwards	**Ends**	McGowan, Bryant, Williams, Farrington
Williams, Hegger, Ellis	**Tackles**	Price, Harris, Means Campbell
Sewell, Ford, Hayes, Reese	**Guards**	Scott, Patterson, Smith
Smith	**Centers**	Robbins, Wilkerson
Henry, Jones, Dunham Howard, Merrel, Walker	**Backs**	Mitchell, Lewis, Scott, Moore, Davis, Powell,

Bryant, Ashley, Chambers   Figures

The Houston Post (November 27, 1953)

1954 LINE-UPS

Wheatley	Position	Yates
Carlton Bell	LE	Bo Farrington
Ellis	LT	Don Franklin
Hayes	LG	Ivory Jones
Smith	C	Wilkerson
McIntosh	RG	Stephens
Sewell	RT	Price
Goffney	RE	Robbins
Cyrus Lancaster	Q	Willie Wheat
Robert Jackson	LH	Thornwell Lewis
Samuel Boudreaux	RH	Chancer Rideaux
Jimmy Bigham	FB	Calvin (The Great) Scott

The Houston Post (November 25, 1954)

1955 LINE-UPS

Wheatley	Position	Yates
Richard Holloway	LE	Powell Dockery
Arthur Sewell	LT	Ivory Jones
Jerry Gibson	LG	James Patterson
Earl Carr	C	Elwood Wilkerson
Wilbert Boson	RG	Andrew Stephens
George Balthazar	RT	Calvin Bass
Arthur Moore	RE	Alfred Henderson
Cyrus Lancaster	QB	David Webster
Henry Williams	LH	Chaucer Rideaux
Robert Jackson	RH	Thornwell Lewis
Everett Bedford	FB	Jerry Jenkins

The Houston Post (November 24, 1955)

1956 LINE-UPS

Wheatley	Position	Yates
Richard Holloway	End	Powell Dockery
Gilbert Dixon	End	John Elder
Aaron Jackson	Center	Richard Robbins
Douglas Lee	Guard	Joseph Autry
R C Stewart	Guard	Julius Hastings
George Balthazar	Tackle	Percy Pittman
Charles Toliver	Tackle	John Solomon
Van Johnson	Back	Donald Dickson
Leonard Charles	Back	Herman Waddy
Charles Jefferson	Back	Sammy Taylor
Cyrus Lancaster	Quarterback	Ivory Jones

The Houston Informer (December 1, 1956)

1957 LINE-UPS

Wheatley	Position	Yates
Andrew Stewart	LE	John Elder
Vernon Mills	LT	Johnnie McKee
Gilbert Dixon	LG	George Boniaby
Herbert Broussard	C	Ronald Bell
Charles Taylor	RG	Julius Hastings
Johnnie Gant	RT	Joseph Autery
Charles Williams	RE	William Gilmore
Raymond Hall	QB	Sammy Taylor
Clarence Steele	LH	Donald Dickson
Donald Ashley	RH	John Marshall
James Taylor	FB	Powell Dockery

The Houston Post (November 28, 1957)

1958 LINE-UPS

Wheatley	Position	Yates
Sidney Williams	RE	David Harris
John Johnson	RT	Sam Smith
Lendon Ashley	RG	Walter Ford
Herbert Broussard	C	William Bradley
Charles Taylor	LG	Curtis Burns
Solomon Ladour	LT	Alphonse Dotson
Charles Williams	LE	Marcus Mosley
Raymond Hall	QB	Jerald Valier
Clarence Steele	RH	Thomas Edwards
Limuel Cox	LH	John Marshall
Joseph McNeal	FB	Cleburne Stephens

The Houston Post (November 27, 1958)

Outstanding players

Yates—Ford, Marshall, Dotson, Hurst

Wheatley—Taylor, Broussard, La Doux

1960—Outstanding players

Yates—Lawrence Dudley, James Johnson

Wheatley—Cullen Johnson, Oris Green, Marbert Montgomery,

Willie Thomas, Eddie Henry, Earl Briggs, Clyde Canada, Green Newman.

1961—Yates—Won the Bi-district game against Hebert of Beaumont

Lost the state contest 19-13 to Anderson High of Austin.

1963 LINE-UPS

Wheatley	Position	Yates
Leo Johnson	End	Thurman Thomas
Edward Haverly	End	William Martin
Hubert Hamilton	Tackle	Norman Calhoun
Andrew Clifton	Tackle	Coger Coverson
Willie Watson	Guard	Irvin Prince
Leroy Johnson	Guard	Cornelius Collins
Harold Washington	Center	Geary Hancock
David Edgely	Quarterback	Lionel Williams
Andrew Blanks	Back	Edwin Nixon
Calvin Fuller	Back	Tedford Sanders
Charles Jones	Fullback	Eddie Hughes

The Houston Post (November 28, 1963)

Outstanding players

> **Yates**—James Rector, Donald Lane, David Stewart, Morgan
> Hunt, Leonard Kirk, Grady Cavness, Larry Guliex.
> **Wheatley**—Gatson Leeland, Harold Hempstead, Willie
> Johnson, Clifton Scott, and Robert Shaw.

1964 LINE-UPS

Wheatley	Position	Yates
Jerald Roberson	Quarterback	Grady Cavness
Andrew Blanks	Back	Clarence Cooper
Joseph Hoskins	End	Robinson Parson
Robert Williams	Back	Phelion Curry
Jake Morris	Back	Norman Calhoun
Thomas Hooper	Center	David Stewart
Darrell Carroll	Guard	Lucius Blair
Leroy Johnson	Tackle	Roy Thomas

Joseph Harris	Tackle	Donald Lang
Simon Smith	End	Lionel Williams
	Back	Richard Lewis

The Houston Informer (November 28, 1964)

1965—Outstanding players
Yates—Leo Taylor, Major Stevenson
Wheatley—Harold Vans, Thomas Hooper, Billy Young, William Henderson

1966 LINE-UPS

Wheatley	**Position**	**Yates**
Jerald Brown	Left End	Robinson Parson
Arthur Scott	Left Tackle	Marion Fletcher
Robert Sherman	Left Guard	Adam Vital
O. Z. White	Center	Phelion Curry
Joel Williams	Right Guard	Emil Glenn
Walter Turk	Right Tackle	M. Lewis
Grady Richardson	Right End	Bobby Blanchard
Huzzell Allen	Quarterback	Leo Taylor
Charles Thomas	Left Halfback	Kenneth Williams
Kenneth Clark	Right Halfback	Ronald Reed
Thomas Wallace	Fullback	George Fountain

The Houston Informer (November 26, 1966)

Head Football Coaches

The head football coaches at Wheatley from 1927 to 1966 included Dr. John Codwell, Obie Williams, Rutherford A. Countee, and Frank Walker in that order.

The head football coaches at Yates from 1926 to 1966 included William Holland, Roger Lights, Develous Johnson and Pat Patterson.